Beyond Land: Exploring Ionospheric Scintillation in the South Atlantic with a Mobile GNSS Receiver

Shivani

1 Introduction 1

1.1 Purpose of the Research . . . .

1.2 Research Objectives . . . .

1.3 Structure of the book . . . .

2 Background 4

2.1 The Ionosphere . . . .

    2.1.1 Introduction to the Ionosphere . . . .

    2.1.2 The Layers of the Ionosphere . . . .

2.2 The South Atlantic Magnetic Anomaly (SAMA) . . . .

2.3 Ionospheric Scintillation . . . .

    2.3.1 Introduction to Ionospheric Scintillation . . . .

    2.3.2 Scale Size and Motion of Ionospheric Irregularities . . . .

    2.3.3 Latitudinal Variances in Scintillation . . . .

    2.3.4 Amplitude Scintillation Index (S_4) . . . .

    2.3.5 Phase Scintillation Index (σ_ϕ) . . . .

2.4 Total Electron Content (TEC) . . . .

2.5 The Global Positioning System (GPS) . . . .

    2.5.1 Introduction to GPS . . . .

    2.5.2 GPS Lock Time . . . .

    2.5.3 Carrier-to-Noise-Density Ratio (C/N_o) . . . .

    2.5.4 Multipath and Multipath Errors . . .

    2.5.5 Theoretical Visibility of GPS Satellites . . . .

    2.5.6 Dilution Of Precision (DOP) . . . .

    2.5.7 Other sources of GPS errors . . . .

2.6 The SA Agulhas II . . . .

2.7 Gough Island . . . .

2.8 Ionospheric Pierce Points (IPP) . . . .

TABLE OF CONTENTS

    2.9   Geomagnetic storms and SYM-H . . . .

3   Data Acquisition   **36**

    3.1   Availability of Data . . . .

    3.2   Hardware: NovAtel GISTM and Antenna . . . .

    3.3   The Multipath Error Roll Tolerance of the SA Agulhas II . . . .

    3.4   Data Recording Software . . . .

        3.4.1   Logger Software: GPS-SCINDA . . . .

        3.4.2   The ISM Binary Data File . . . .

        3.4.3   The PSN Data File . . . .

    3.5   Data Problems and Corrections . . . .

        3.5.1   GPS Epoch Corrections . . . .

        3.5.2   UTC and SAST Misalignment . . . .

4   Data Analysis   **47**

    4.1   Thresholds . . . .

        4.1.1   Multipath error thresholds . . . .

        4.1.2   Scintillation thresholds . . . .

        4.1.3   Threshold values for daily scintillation count histograms . . . .

        4.1.4   Threshold values for MATLAB scintillation analysis . . . .

    4.2   Daily scintillation count histograms (SA Agulhas II data) . . . .

        4.2.1   Daily histogram pattern analysis: SA Agulhas II . . . .

    4.3   Geographic and time constraints . . . .

    4.4   Histogram comparison: Gough Island and SA Agulhas II . . . .

    4.5   MATLAB Analysis: ISM and PSN output graphs . . . .

        4.5.1   Plot ID 1: Carrier-to-Noise Density ratio (C/N_o) . . . .

        4.5.2   Plot ID 2: L1 Lock Time and Elevation (all PRN) graphs

        4.5.3   Plot ID 3: L1 Lock Time and Elevation (single PRN) graphs . . . .

        4.5.4   Plot ID 10: Raw S_4 (all PRN) graphs . . . .

        4.5.5   Plot ID 11: Elevation vs S_{4c} multi-pane (all PRN) graphs . . . .

        4.5.6   Plot ID 13: Corrected S_{4c} (all PRN) graphs . . . .

        4.5.7   Plot ID 20: Raw σ_ϕ (all PRN) graphs . . . .

        4.5.8   Plot ID 22: Elevation vs. σ_ϕ multi-pane (all PRN) graphs . . . .

        4.5.9   Plot ID 23: Corrected σ_ϕ (all PRN) graphs . . . .

        4.5.10 Plot ID 24: Corrected σ_ϕ (single PRN) graphs . . . .

        4.5.11   Plot ID 25: Corrected S_{4c} (single PRN) graphs . . . .

        4.5.12   Plot ID 30: Slant TEC (all PRN) graphs . . . .

        4.5.13   Plot ID 31: Vertical TEC (all PRN) graphs . . . .

        4.5.14   Plot ID 50: GPS Satellite Visibility (all PRN) graphs . . . .

        4.5.15   Plot ID 58: Instantaneous Velocity graphs . . . .

        4.5.16   Plot ID 87: Horizontal Error and Locked Satellites graphs

        4.5.17   Plot ID 88: SA Agulhas II and Gough Island GISTM Trajectory graphs

        4.5.18   Plot ID 991: Horizontal Position Error Distribution graphs . . . .

        4.5.19   Plot ID 992: Vertical Position Error Distribution graphs . . . .

4.5.20   Plot ID 993: Absolute Position Error Distribution graphs . . . .

4.5.21   Plot ID 994: Variation in Latitude, Longitude and Altitude graphs . . . .

4.5.22   Plot ID 995: Running Mean Error graphs . . . .

4.5.23   Plot ID 996: Latitude-Longitude Scatter Plot . . . .

4.5.24   Plot ID 997: X-Y Position Estimate Scatter Plot . . . .

4.6   Calculation of position accuracy . . . .

4.7   Filtering of Motion Noise . . . .

5   Results and Discussion   96

5.1   Daily scintillation count histograms . . . .

5.2   Motion-induced scintillation noise . . . .

5.3   Gough Island scintillation observations . . . .

5.4   SYM-H geomagnetic storm index . . . .

5.5 Identification of scintillation by other proxies . . . .

5.6   The effects of noise on position accuracy . . . .

5.7   The effect of satellite availability on position error. . . . .

5.8   Recurring C/N_o fades and loss of lock in PRN32 . . . .

5.9 Identification of additional noise sources . . . .

6   Conclusions   116

6.1   Objectives achieved . . . .

6.2 Unique findings . . . .

6.3   Research Outcomes . . . .

6.4   Future work . . . .

A   Appendix A   121

A.1   Scripting . . . .

A.1.1   PSN Concatenation Script . . . .

A.1.2   ISM Concatenation & Plotting Script . . . .

A.1.3   Daily Histogram Script . . . .

A.1.4   Ruby Data File Correction Script . . . .

A.2   MATLAB Code Overview . . . .

A.2.1   MATLAB: ISM scripts . . . .

A.2.2   MATLAB: PSN scripts . . . .

References   133

Ionospheric scintillation is a physical phenomenon which presents as rapid fluctuations in the phase and amplitude of trans-ionospheric radio signals. These fluctuations have the potential to degrade the accuracy of space-based navigation systems, as well as affect general radio communications with satellites in orbit around Earth. The fluctuations can occur in one of two ways: Phase scintillation (Sigma Phi, σ_ϕ) is distinguishable as rapid changes in the phase of the carrier wave, while amplitude scintillation (S-four, S_4) presents as an abrupt and severe fade in the strength of the radio signal.

In the application of Global Navigation Satellite Systems (GNSSs), scintillation can cause a loss of signal lock between the ground-based receiver and the transmitting satellite. This in turn can increase position errors (Doherty et al., 2003) This is a serious risk factor for many modern aircraft and ocean vessels which rely heavily on GNSS for access to accurate Position, Navigation and Timing (PNT) services in order to operate safely. This research undertakes the novel comparison of scintillation data at the L1 frequency sampled at 50 Hz from a mobile GPS Ionospheric Scintillation and Total Electron Content Monitor (GISTM), located on board the polar research vessel SA Agulhas II, with data from a stationary GISTM on Gough Island, to investigate the prevalence of ionospheric scintillation in the South Atlantic Magnetic Anomaly (SAMA). Previously, the analysis of GISTM data involved only stationary receivers.

This book reports on the the hardware, software, challenges, solutions, and constraints involved in the analysis of the first ship-based terrestrial measurements of scintillation indices from locations in the SAMA which were previously beyond the reach of land-based receivers.

1.1 Purpose of the Research

The purpose of this research was the first analysis of the method and measurements of ionospheric scintillation using a ship-based receiver within the SAMA.

The SAMA is an under-explored region with unusual magnetic properties. Whilst it can easily be mapped and monitored from space, it is much harder to study using terrestrial equipment. This is largely owing to the fact that the SAMA is mostly ocean, which requires the use of seafaring vessels or the presence of islands in order to conduct terrestrial studies.

In order to study the effect of ionospheric scintillation on radio signals which pass through the atmosphere from satellites to the ground, it is necessary to utilise receivers of a terrestrial nature. Space-based studies cannot determine the variances produced in trans-ionospheric signals at a terrestrial level. However, the number of islands within the SAMA which allow for terrestrial studies to be conducted is minimal. The range of fixed terrestrial receivers is also not large enough to span the extent necessary to properly study the entire area of the SAMA.

Ionospheric scintillation, especially in the presence of magnetic storm activity, can have a great influence on the phase and amplitude of radio signals. In the case of the Global Positioning System (GPS), in which these signals are used to accurately determine location and movement of the receiver, any form of fluctuation can result in a loss of precision. For the individual end user of a PNT system, accuracy is not as critical as it is for military or commercial applications. A 20 m position variation is acceptable when navigating to the nearest shopping centre, but is unacceptable for a crewed passenger aircraft using GPS-guided autopilot to land on a runway in bad weather.

Scintillation is not well understood at mid-latitudes, and as stated before, the unusual magnetic conditions of the SAMA are also not well-studied. The combination of these two factors in one region is thus of great scientific interest.

It has been shown that significantly accurate studies of scintillation are possible whilst using a moving receiver (van der Merwe, 2011). Thus in 2012 the South African National Space Agency (SANSA) undertook the installation of a GISTM aboard the SA Agulhas II, which traverses the eastern edge of the SAMA during its annual voyages through the southern oceans. This receiver was left to record data for almost 4 years before the first analysis of the recorded data could be conducted. This book is the result of that analysis.

This research initially intended to identify scintillation within the SAMA and determine whether it is possible to map the structures in the ionosphere over the SAMA using the data obtained from a moving receiver. However, the project rapidly evolved into a more technical assessment of the challenges encountered in using a moving receiver of its specific type aboard the vessel in question, whilst retaining the goal of attempting to identify any instances of scintillation within the SAMA in the recorded data.

The data files presented a significant processing challenge before their content could be of any use. Problems such as missing time periods, misaligned dates, incorrect receiver settings, proprietary data formats, and outdated processing software all had to be investigated and resolved. The data underwent significant pre-processing and testing to ensure the integrity of the data had been retained, before it could be used for the scientific analysis presented in this book.

1.2 Research Objectives

The technical challenges and objectives of this project were:

1. Determining the causes, extent of, and solutions to, the NovAtel receiver's configuration and data problems.

2. Updating the processing scripts which were needed to convert the data to accessible formats and group them into appropriate time spans.

3. Investigate and prove the effect of receiver motion on the data.

4. Test the geometric limitations of the receiver platform to ensure that no additional factors are contributing to noise in the recorded data.

5. Determine whether the noise from motion effects can be removed using frequency response analysis.

6. Develop the analysis software needed to process the scintillation and GPS data from a moving receiver.

7. Show whether the receiver was able to detect scintillation despite motion noise effects.

8. Compare the moving receiver data to stationary receiver data to test the fidelity of the results obtained.

9. Assess the overall accuracy of the moving receiver data under the effects of motion noise and ionospheric scintillation.

1.3 Structure of the book

Chapter 2 introduces the necessary theoretical background of all the technical and scientific aspects of the research. Chapter 3 delves into the detail of the hardware and software involved in the acquisition and processing of the data, as well as the steps taken to resolve the multiple data issues that were experienced.

Chapter 4 explains the methods used to perform the analysis of the data, and clarifies the various constraints and thresholds which were applied during the analysis. Chapter 5 discusses the results that were obtained from the various analyses.

Chapter 6 presents the conclusions that were drawn from this work, and highlights a number of potential future projects which may result from, or make use of this work.

In order to fulfil the objectives of this research it is important to first have a clear understanding of the physical context as well as the unique environment in which the work takes place. This chapter provides the theoretical context for the various technical and scientific aspects pertaining to this research.

These aspects include ionospheric scintillation, the GPS satellite constellation, the South Atlantic Magnetic Anomaly (SAMA), the SA Agulhas II polar research vessel, as well as important physical factors which had to be taken into consideration during the execution of this project.

The structure of the ionosphere as well as the propagation of radio waves through this region are described. Scintillation as a phenomenon is dependent on a variety of factors, and varies greatly with geography. The SAMA is a region of particular interest for ionospheric scintillation because of the weakened magnetic field in this area. As the central focus of this research, the methods for identifying and measuring ionospheric scintillation as well as the causes thereof should be thoroughly studied. Other measurements of the ionosphere which have relevance to scintillation, such as Total Electron Content (TEC), must also be understood.

This research makes use of data sourced only from GPS satellites. GPS is a highly sophisticated space system with its own limitations and operational factors. Concepts such as satellite identification, trilateration, operating frequencies, ionospheric delay correction models, lock time, carrier-to-noise density ratios, accessibility, and potential causes of irregularities, such as multipath and dilution of precision, are discussed.

A brief introduction to the SA Agulhas II research ship is included, as well as Gough Island, as these are the two location platforms utilised for the receiver, each with its own environmental challenges. Lastly, we discuss geomagnetic storms and their measurement, as this is an external factor which can affect the conditions under which data is recorded.

2.1   The Ionosphere

2.1.1   Introduction to the Ionosphere

The ionosphere is a region of charged particles which spans across the mesosphere, thermosphere and exosphere layers of the Earth's atmosphere between 50–1000 km as seen in Figure 2.1. The lower atmosphere, below the ozone layer (~45 km), is neutral in charge. The upper layers of the atmosphere, above the ozone layer, are ionised and exhibit conductive behaviour. Many free electrons are present here, produced when radiation from the Sun causes photo-ionisation of molecules and atoms.

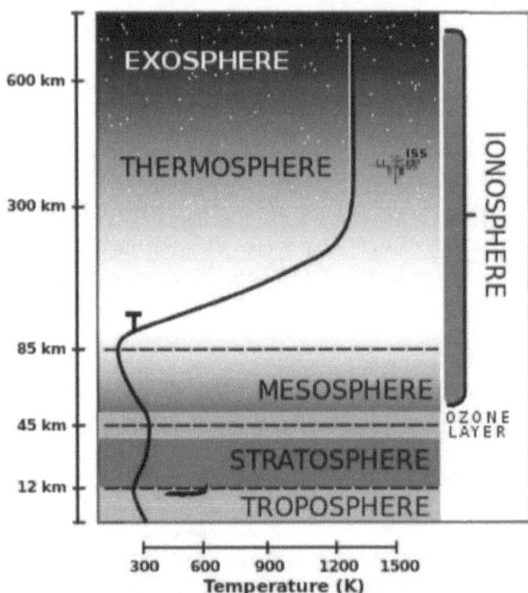

Figure 2.1: Schematic of the layers of the atmosphere and the ionosphere. Atmospheric layers are defined according to changes in temperature. The ionosphere extends up to an altitude of 1000 km.

The rate at which free electrons are produced is determined by both the number of available neutral atoms and the intensity of solar photons. The ionised layers above the ozone layer have the greatest effect on trans-ionospheric radio signals from satellites which are used for navigation or communication purposes (McNamara, 1991).

The density of the free electrons, measured in electrons per m^3, varies according to the 11-year solar cycle, diurnal and seasonal factors, as well as geography (Georges, 1969). These free electrons are responsible for the refraction of radio waves within the ionosphere, as well as the reflection of radio waves off the ionosphere. Terrestrial radio communication takes advantage of this unique characteristic by using the ionosphere to bounce radio signals back down to Earth, thereby allowing for ground-to-ground radio communication over large distances and even around the curvature of the Earth.

The critical frequency (f_c) at which a radio signal will still be reflected off the ionosphere depends on the electron density (N) of the ionosphere. It is calculated using the plasma frequency (f_N), the angular frequency (ω), electron mass (m), the permittivity of free space (ϵ_0), and the mass of an electron (m) as shown in Equations 2.1 through 2.4 (McNamara, 1991).

$$f_N = \omega/2\pi \tag{2.1}$$

$$\omega = Ne^2/\epsilon_0 m \tag{2.2}$$

$$f_N = \frac{e}{2\pi(\epsilon_0 m)^{1/2}} N^{1/2} \tag{2.3}$$

Using $m_e = 9.11 \times 10^{-31}$ kg, $\epsilon_0 = 8.854 \times 10^{-12}$ Fm^{-1}, and $e = 1.602 \times 10^{-19}$ C, the relation between the maximum critical frequency (in MHz) and maximum electron density (in e/m^3) is:

$$f_c \approx 9 \times 10^{-6} N_m^{1/2} \tag{2.4}$$

2.1.2 The Layers of the Ionosphere

The ionosphere comprises four layers, identified by their level of ionization. The lowest layer is called the D-layer and lies between 50 and 90 km. The D-layer reflects Extremely Low Frequency (ELF) and Very Low Frequency (VLF) radio waves. It is also responsible for the absorption of the lower High Frequency (HF) radio waves. This property causes long-distance HF radio transmissions to degrade. The D-layer is highly dependent on Ultraviolet (UV) radiation from the sun to remain ionised, and in the absence of this driver it disappears.

The second layer lies between 90 and 140 km and is called the E-layer. It has a peak electron density on the order of 100 times greater than the D-layer. The E-layer also fades away in the absence of photo-ionisation from the sun. Both of these layers primarily experience molecular ionisation (McNamara, 1991). Figure 2.2 shows the various layers of the ionosphere and the difference in structure between daytime and nighttime.

The two upper layers of the ionosphere are known as the $F1$ (inner) and $F2$ (outer) layers. Together these are simply known as the F-layer. It lies between 140–1000 km, and primarily experiences atomic ionisation rather than molecular ionisation. The $F2$-layer has a higher electron density than the $F1$-layer. The $F1$-layer also disappears in the absence of photo-ionisation. The $F2$-layer thins out and shifts upwards during the night but remains present and can still be used to bounce long-distance HF radio transmissions (McNamara, 1991).

This research deals specifically with ionospheric scintillation, which occurs when the electron density varies rapidly. As there is a direct link between electron density and the critical frequency, changes in N lead to changes in f_c. In the case of trans-ionospheric radio waves, the signal penetrates through the layers

Figure 2.2: All four layers of the ionosphere, D,E,F1 and F2, are present during the day. At night, the D, E and F1 layers dissipate. Only the thinned F layer remains.

of the ionosphere instead of being reflected off it. This is possible while the transmission frequency is greater than the critical frequency of the $F2$-layer. Frequencies below $f_{c(F2)}$ will reflect, while frequencies above $f_{c(F2)}$ can pass through.

2.2 The South Atlantic Magnetic Anomaly (SAMA)

The South Atlantic Magnetic Anomaly (SAMA) is a region in the South Atlantic Ocean where the Earth's magnetic field is weakest. It is up to 60% weaker here than elsewhere at comparable latitudes (Korte et al., 2009). The reduced protection provided by the weakened magnetic field results in an increased proton flux due to precipitation of high-energy particles from the Van Allen radiation belts into the ionosphere during geomagnetic storms (van der Merwe, 2011). High-energy particle precipitation over the SAMA is known to affect the electronics of satellites in Low Earth Orbit (LEO). Precipitation also results in electron density variations along the ray path which cause interference in trans-ionospheric radio signals (Kintner et al., 2009).

The extent of the SAMA can be defined in a number of different ways: by proton flux, by the magnetic field intensity, by the number of incidents of satellite anomalies, or by the level of particle precipitation. A gradient map showing the extent of the SAMA, as defined in terms of proton flux values exceeding 50 MeV at an altitude of 500 km, is shown in Figure 2.3.

The majority of data source sites chosen for use in this research were all located at, or close to Gough Island. The location of Gough Island is scientifically valuable because it is situated close to the centre of the SAMA and is accessible for research teams and the permanent installation of equipment. It therefore provides a higher likelihood of observing scintillation within the SAMA than elsewhere at similar latitudes.

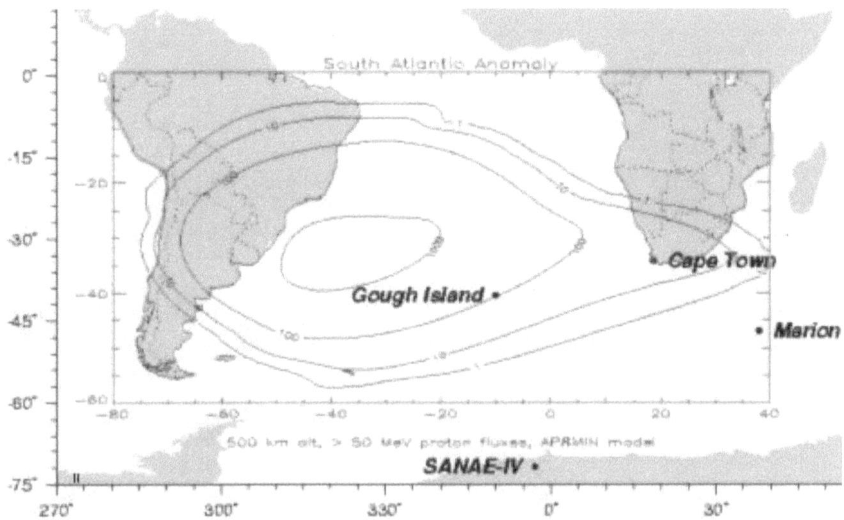

Figure 2.3: The South Atlantic Magnetic Anomaly is defined in terms of proton flux particles with energies > 50 MeV at an altitude of 500 km (Cilliers et al., 2006).

More detail about Gough Island is available in Section 2.7.

Field intensity measurements for the Earth's geomagnetic field have been recorded since the 1840s. Before this, only directional field data was available. With the use of models such as the International Geomagnetic Reference Field (IGRF), field intensity maps have been created going back as far as 1590 as shown in Figure 2.4. These maps show that the SAMA is experiencing a gradual westward drift and that the field strength has been decreasing steadily, thereby expanding the range of influence of the SAMA (Hartmann and Pacca, 2009).

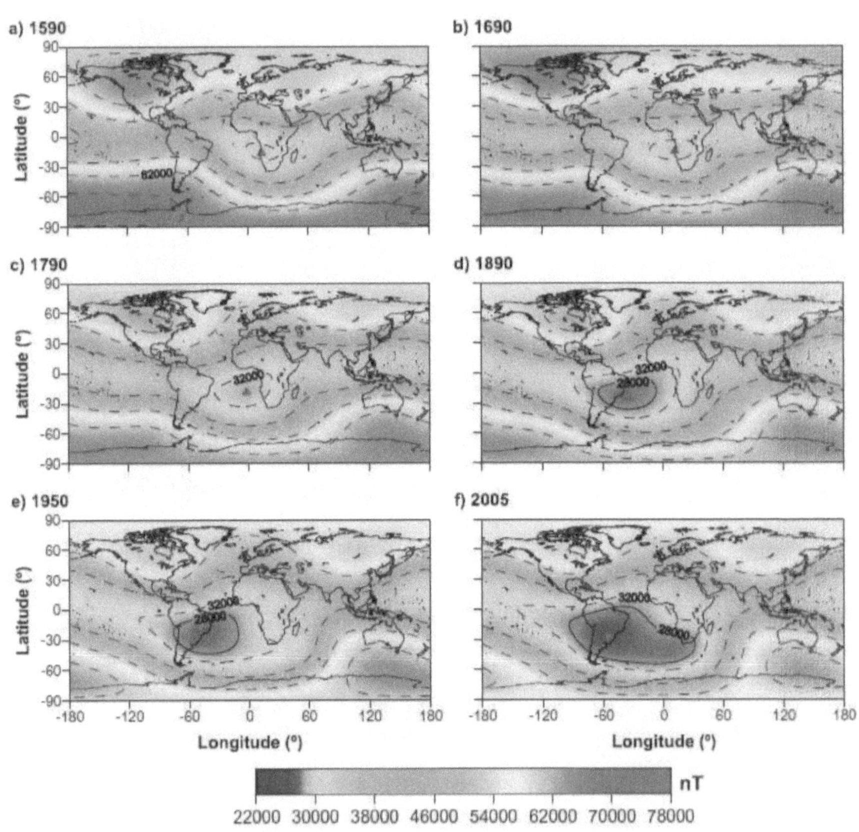

Figure 2.4: Geomagnetic field intensity maps of the SAMA created using the *gufm1* and IGRF models show the westward drift, decreasing field strength, and increasing extent of the SAMA, over a 415-year period. The red triangle indicates the centre of the SAMA (Hartmann and Pacca, 2009).

2.3 Ionospheric Scintillation

2.3.1 Introduction to Ionospheric Scintillation

Ionospheric scintillation is measurable as rapid fluctuations in the amplitude and phase of trans-ionospheric radio signals. Amplitude scintillation is rapid variations in the power levels of the radio signals. If this variation is severe enough that the signal level drops below the threshold required to maintain the connection to the satellite then this is termed *Loss of Lock* (Carrano et al., 2005).

Phase scintillation generally presents as rapid fluctuations in the carrier phase, and can result in increased phase noise, cycle slips, or even loss of lock when the fluctuations are too rapid to be tracked by the GPS receiver. Scintillation is dependent on many factors. It can vary because of the 11-year solar cycle, geomagnetic storm conditions, time of day, season, latitude and signal frequency. Scintillation activity is rare at mid-latitudes and usually occurs only when a strong geomagnetic storm is present (Doherty et al., 2003).

Rapid variations in the electron density of the ionosphere causes irregularities in the index of refraction that result in amplitude scintillation. The radio signal is scattered in random directions which centre about the original direction of propagation. The signal can be redirected multiple times, and may even cause interference with itself through either constructive or destructive wave interference. The signal can either be attenuated or reinforced by this interference, however the average power received by the user remains unchanged as short, intense fades are offset by longer, weaker enhancements (SBAS Ionospheric Working Group, 2010).

The physical mechanisms which govern the formation and evolution of these irregularities have been extensively studied and documented in many papers and textbooks, such as Wernik et al. (2003) and the references therein. The majority of these studies have been conducted for equatorial regions (Aarons, 1993) or at high latitudes (SBAS Ionospheric Working Group, 2010), as the drivers of scintillation in these two zones differ greatly. The SAMA is located at mid-latitudes which have not been as extensively studied.

As shown by Equation 2.4 in Section 2.1, a direct relationship exists between the critical frequency and the electron density. When rapid variations in electron density occur, the critical frequency will also fluctuate rapidly in response. Scintillation is therefore frequency-dependent. A dual-frequency system allows for one frequency to be affected by scintillation while the other is not. The greater the distance between the two transmission frequencies, the less likely it is that the fluctuation in critical frequency can encompass both.

2.3.2 Scale Size and Motion of Ionospheric Irregularities

Radio waves which pass through the ionosphere can be scattered because of varying electron density, and the scattered wave fronts can interact with each other and the original signal in both destructive and constructive ways. The ionosphere is not, however, a single thin layer with homogeneous behaviour.

Electron density variations which cause changes in the index of refraction can take place in both the horizontal and vertical planes, and even vary within each layer of the ionosphere. Irregularities are classified either as 'bubbles', which are areas where the electron density is depleted, or 'patches', which are high electron density zones. In equatorial regions, the majority of irregularities can be found between 200-400 km in altitude (Aarons, 1993). This coincides with the F-layer of the ionosphere.

Models of the irregularities which produce scintillation do exist for the mid-latitudes. One example is the 35°-45° WBMOD model which was based on data from the Defense Nuclear Agency (DNA) Wideband and Hilat satellites (Robins et al., 1986). A comparison of the model against empirical data showed that the E-layer contributes strongly towards daytime scintillations, while nighttime scintillations are produced by the F-layer.

The irregularities are not stationary within the ionosphere, and experience an easterly drift at night, and a westward drift during the day (Robins et al., 1986). The movement of the scintillation-producing irregularities, combined with the rapid orbital motion of GPS satellites results in very short periods during which trans-ionospheric radio signals can experience scintillation. The drift velocity can vary between 100-180 ms^{-1} depending on time of year and solar activity. As solar flux decreases, so does the mean velocity of the irregularities (Muella et al., 2014).

However, the SA Agulhas II (see Section 2.6 for detail) is also in motion during its voyages through the SAMA. Both the magnitude of the zonal drift velocity of the ionospheric irregularities as well as the speed of the GPS satellites across the sky far outweigh the motion of the SA Agulhas II. The ship's average cruising speed in ideal ocean conditions is 13 kts ($\sim 6.7\ ms^{-1}$). As a result, the speed of the SA Agulhas II is ignored as a contributor to the duration of scintillations recorded by its GISTM.

It has been shown that the scale of an ionospheric irregularity has a direct relation to the frequencies which it can disrupt. The scale size of irregularities which cause problems for L1 (1.575 GHz) are on the order of 370-400 m, depending on the altitude of the irregularity layer (360-420 km). By contrast, the irregularities which affect VHF are on the order of a kilometre in size (Muella et al., 2014).

This scale, known as the Fresnel zone radius (r), is dependent on the distance between the receiver and the plane of the irregularity (h), as well as on the wavelength (λ) of the radio signal, in the form $r = \sqrt{h\lambda}$. The GPS L1 frequency has a wavelength of $\lambda = 19$ cm. Fresnel zones are schematically depicted as a series of concentric circles for which the distance h (to the receiver) of the outer edge of each successive circle (Fresnel zone) increases by $\lambda/2$ (Rawer, 1993).

Radio signals which pass through irregularities that have a scale length smaller than the size of the first Fresnel zone can only experience changes to their phase. If the irregularity is larger than the first Fresnel zone, the signal can show scintillations in both phase and amplitude. Lastly, it is important to note that smaller irregularities tend to have lower drift velocities than large-scale irregularities (Muella et al., 2014).

2.3.3 Latitudinal Variances in Scintillation

Scintillation is known to vary by latitude (as well as longitude). The equatorial regions (low latitudes) encounter these effects most frequently, while the polar regions experience scintillation less frequently than the low-latitudes, as shown in Figure 2.5. The instances of scintillation decrease dramatically in the mid-latitudes. The marked distortion of the bands in the mid-latitude area between South America and Southern Africa coincides with the location of the SAMA.

The low latitudes (equatorial regions) are defined as the zone between $15°N$ to $15°S$ of the magnetic equator. This area is well known for its greater variability in ionospheric delay as the structure of the ionosphere is more unstable as a result of the Rayleigh-Taylor instability at the magnetic equator. Large-scale plasma bubbles develop many smaller irregularities which cause intense scintillation as the low-density bubbles move upwards (Basu et al., 2002). As a result, amplitude and phase scintillation are much stronger and occur more regularly in this region, and can be a nearly daily event during solar maximum. Scintillation is primarily observed between sunset and midnight (local time) (SBAS Ionospheric Working Group, 2010).

The high-latitudes consist of two zones. The auroral region is defined as the high-latitude zone centred around the 60° latitude line. The primary mechanism which drives scintillation in the auroral regions is the formation of high-density patches caused by an increase in the precipitation of high-energy particles from the Van Allen radiation belts (Kintner et al., 2009).

Scintillation in this region is associated with the aurora, as the precipitation of high-energy electrons occurs along the Earth's magnetic field lines. The interaction between these highly energised particles and atmospheric molecules result in the colourful light emissions known as the Aurora Borealis (Northern Lights) or Aurora Australis (Southern Lights) (Skone et al., 2001).

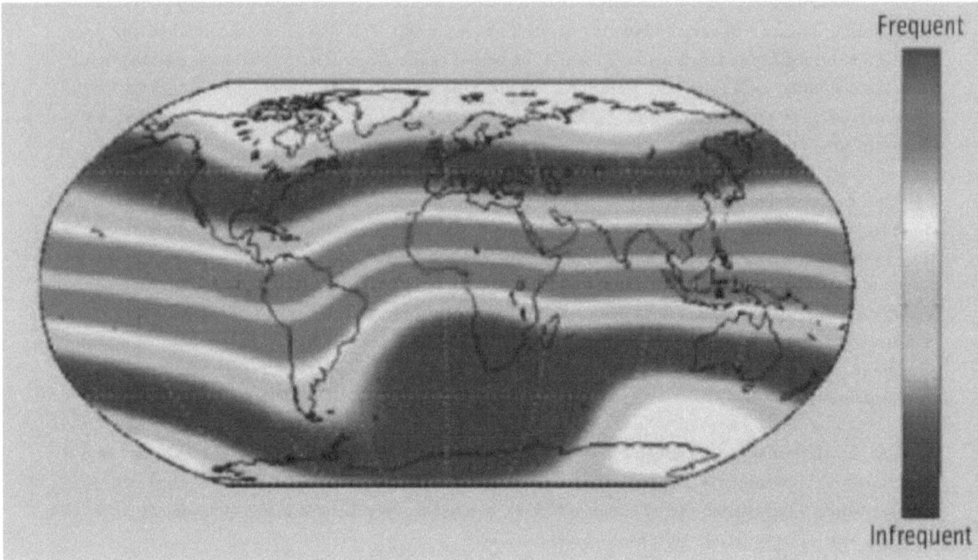

Figure 2.5: Global map of the frequency of ionospheric scintillation disturbances during solar maximum. The equatorial, mid-latitude and polar zones are clearly visible. Scintillation is most frequent and intense in the two zones adjacent to the magnetic equator. It can occur up to 100 days in a year (Kintner et al., 2009). The distortion of the equatorial and mid-latitude bands between Africa and South America coincides with the location of the SAMA.

The polar region is the zone of latitude >75° and is associated with the polar caps. During the winter months when the sun is permanently below the horizon, scintillations in the polar region become more intense and are generally as a result of high-density patches. The formation mechanism of these patches, and the interaction of the polar zone with the auroral zone, depends on the direction of the Interplanetary Magnetic Field (IMF). However, at these high latitudes, scintillation tends to occur at any time of day and in all seasons, and is strongly affected by geomagnetic storm activity (Basu et al., 2002).

Amplitude scintillations at high latitudes tend to produce somewhat weaker signal fades than in the equatorial zone, while phase scintillations in the high latitudes can be equal to or stronger than those recorded in the low latitudes (SBAS Ionospheric Working Group, 2010). The polar region has been observed to experience more intense signal fades than the auroral region (Doherty et al., 2003).

The zone of interest for this research, the mid-latitudes, lies between 15°-45° (N and S), centred around the 30° latitude line. The mid-latitude ionosphere is known to have more gradual latitudinal TEC gradients than either the low-latitude or high-latitude areas. The smooth nature of the ionosphere in the mid-latitudes contributes to lower levels of scintillation. It is thus expected that scintillation will be rarer in the mid-latitudes than in the auroral and equatorial regions (SBAS Ionospheric Working Group, 2010).

However, the SAMA is a magnetically weak zone within the mid-latitudes which allows for higher levels of high-energy particle precipitation, especially during geomagnetic storms. This may create electron density variations that can result in scintillation, and is the basis for the hypothesis that scintillation might occur more regularly within the SAMA than outside the SAMA at similar latitudes.

Despite the physical limitations and accompanying lack of available data from within the SAMA region, work has been done to map scintillation using GISTMs located around the periphery of the SAMA. An example is the use of the Ground-Based Scintillation Climatology (GBSC) technique on data from South America and Antarctica, Marion Island and some from Gough Island (Spogli et al., 2013).

2.3.4 Amplitude Scintillation Index (S_4)

Amplitude scintillation is measured using an index denoted 'S_4'. The widely accepted definition of the S_4 index is the *"normalised root mean squared (RMS) deviation of the received signal power intensity"* (see Jiao et al. (2013), Muella et al. (2014), Van Dierendonck et al. (1993), Wang et al. (2016) and many others). The S_4 index is a dimensionless ratio derived from the detrended signal power intensity (I) data recorded by the GISTM at 50 Hz and is expressed as follows:

$$S_4 = \sqrt{\frac{\langle I^2 \rangle - \langle I \rangle^2}{\langle I \rangle^2}} \qquad (2.5)$$

The brackets $\langle \rangle$ represent an average normally taken over a 60 s interval. In some literature, the signal power amplitude P_m (also sometimes denoted by A for amplitude) is used instead of the signal intensity I as the relation between these is simply $I = A^2$ (Muella et al., 2014). S_4 is normalised against the mean signal power, and detrending is usually performed using a 6th-order Butterworth low-pass filter (e.g. Van Dierendonck (2009), Doherty et al. (2003)).

The receiver can also calculate the effect of ambient noise on the measured S_4. This is done over the same period, using the average of the 1 Hz Carrier-to-Noise-Density Ratio (C/N_o), in order to determine a correction factor S_4Cor which is needed to remove the ambient noise effect and produce the corrected S_{4c}. If the correction factor S_4Cor is greater than the total measured raw S_4 then the corrected S_{4c} is set to zero since the raw S_4 value was entirely due to noise. However, if the correction factor S_4Cor is less than the total measured raw S_4, then the corrected S_{4c} is calculated as follows:

$$S_{4c} = \sqrt{S_4^2 - S_4Cor^2} \qquad (2.6)$$

For GNSS-specific receivers, the total S_4 includes the error-inducing effects of ambient receiver noise as well as multipath. These error effects can be distinguished using a separate receiver measurement called the code/carrier divergence. The calculation of C/N_o and the definition of multipath are discussed in sections 2.5.3 and 2.5.4.

Amplitude scintillation of trans-ionospheric radio signals presents as rapid variations (~50 Hz) in the signal intensity. In the equatorial regions, these Signal-to-Noise Ratio (SNR) fades can be as deep as 20 dB below the mean (Doherty et al., 2003). These effects are mainly caused by signal absorption in the ionosphere, as well as attenuation over long distances.

Every receiver has a minimum power intensity threshold required to maintain a signal lock on a transmitter (in this case, a satellite), and when the intensity drops below the threshold the receiver will be unable to retain the connection. Severe scintillation can also prevent a receiver from acquiring an initial lock on a satellite, or delay the re-acquisition of signal from the previously disconnected satellite (Carrano et al., 2005).

2.3.5   Phase Scintillation Index (σ_ϕ)

Phase scintillation is measured using an index denoted 'σ_ϕ'. The σ_ϕ index (measured in radians) is widely defined as the *"standard deviation of the detrended carrier phase"* (see Jiao et al. (2013); Muella et al. (2014); Van Dierendonck et al. (1993); Wang et al. (2016) and many others), and is measured at 50 Hz, typically over the same 60 s interval as the associated amplitude scintillation index S_4. It is calculated as follows:

$$\sigma_\phi = \sqrt{\langle \phi^2 \rangle - \langle \phi \rangle^2} \tag{2.7}$$

As before, the brackets $\langle \ \rangle$ represent an average over the standard 60 s period. σ_ϕ does not require normalisation, and detrending is usually performed using a 6th-order Butterworth high-pass filter (eg. Van Dierendonck (2009); Doherty et al. (2003)) as opposed to the low-pass filter used for S_4 detrending. The previous 3000 detrended phase data points can also be used to calculate the statistics of the residuals, over periods of 1, 3, 10, 30 and 60 seconds, once every minute.

Phase scintillations predominantly result from rapid variations in ionospheric refraction and diffraction effects (Muella et al., 2014). Radio signal receivers make use of a Phase Lock Loop (PLL) to maintain phase with the transmitter. Scintillations in the phase may exceed the ability of the PLL and result in cycle slips and loss of lock (Carrano et al. (2005); NovAtel (2015) and others). However, rapid movements of the antenna at a frequency within the band of the PLL can also cause signal variations that mimic scintillation and mask actual scintillations.

Narrower bandwidths in the PLL provide better tracking performance with lower SNR. However, for receivers specifically designed to study scintillation it is important to have greater resilience to loss of lock, and thus the PLL bandwidths in many GISTMs are increased to provide this enhanced ability to maintain a connection with the satellite in the presence of scintillation.

2.4 Total Electron Content (TEC)

Total Electron Content (TEC) is a parameter that characterises the state of the ionosphere. It describes the ionosphere's level of ionisation. It is used for corrections to navigation system position estimates, and also for ionospheric scintillation proxies.

TEC is defined as the total number of electrons in a cylinder with a cross-sectional area of 1 m^2 centred on the ray path (Hofmann-Wellenhof et al., 2001) and is measured in Total Electron Content Units (TECU). When measured directly along the ray path it is called the Slant Total Electron Content (STEC). The equivalent Vertical Total Electron Content (VTEC) can be derived by scaling the STEC using a mapping function for a specific ionospheric shell height (see Section 2.8). The smoother curves of VTEC facilitate easier identification of errors (Horvath and Crozier, 2007).

TEC has been well-studied and the temporal (diurnal and seasonal) variations and geographic characteristics are well known, even in the mid-latitudes. Other factors which contribute to TEC variation include solar and magnetic activity (Habarulema et al., 2009). TEC behaves in a fairly regular manner, with a global diurnal maximum at 14:00 local time. The standard deviation from the monthly average TEC for any given hour is usually between 20–25% of the mean TEC (Klobuchar, 1987).

Because of the regular behaviour of TEC, most ionospheric correction models for satellite navigation systems are formulated in terms of TEC. Scintillation occurs where there is a rapid variation in the electron density, and a variation in density can also present as a variation in TEC. TEC graphs were generated from the data obtained by the GISTM, as rapid TEC fluctuations typically may signify the presence of scintillation.

TEC-based ionospheric correction models used in GPS are generally based on data from dual-frequency GNSS receivers. These receivers are complex, expensive, and civilian use is currently limited to specific applications such as geodesy or surveying. The majority of commercial aviation presently relies on single-frequency receivers. A 2017 breakthrough in mass-produced low-cost low-energy small dual-frequency (L1 and L5) GNSS chips for use in consumer electronics has the potential to rapidly change the prevalence of dual-frequency receivers (Cozzens, 2017).

The electrons that a radio wave encounters during travel through the ionosphere have the greatest effect on the signal time delay. Single-frequency GPS receivers have an ionospheric time-delay algorithm incorporated in their system which was developed by Klobuchar in 1987. This algorithm is a cosine representation of the TEC diurnal curve. The period and amplitude values in the algorithm vary by the receiver's latitude, and is dependent on the location and local time of the receiver. The algorithm requires 8 coefficients which are received as part of the broadcast navigation message from the satellite on a regular basis. A single-frequency GPS receiver will insert the appropriate coefficients into the algorithm and the necessary corrections are made.

Updates to the coefficients are made once a day to ensure accuracy regarding current space weather conditions under regular behaviour of the ionosphere (Klobuchar, 1987). This error correction method cannot be used during rapid fluctuations in the TEC as a result of scintillation. The magnitude of the error, however, can be estimated from the intensity of the scintillations.

Other methods of characterising scintillation include the use of ionospheric scintillation proxies. Scintillation proxies are parameters which have the same characteristics as the scintillation indices σ_ϕ and S_4 but which are derived from other standard GPS Receiver Independent Exchange Format (RINEX) parameters. Two scintillation proxies which have been shown to accurately mimic the behaviour of scintillation are the Delta Phase Rate (DPR) and the standard deviation of the rate of change of TEC (ROTI).

ROTI is derived from TEC; it can be used to indicate the presence of amplitude scintillations and is related to S_4 (Du et al., 2000). DPR is the rate of change of ionospheric phase (ψ_i) and is derived by statistical examination of the phase difference variations (at 1 Hz) of two GPS frequencies. It is calibrated with respect to σ_ϕ measurements (at 50 Hz) on a single GPS frequency (Ghoddousi-Fard et al., 2013). The DPR and ROTI scintillation proxies were not used in this research.

2.5 The Global Positioning System (GPS)

2.5.1 Introduction to GPS

GPS is one of several GNSS constellations currently operating in Medium Earth Orbit (MEO). It is owned by the United States government and maintained by the United States Air Force (USAF). The GPS constellation is arranged into 24 standard slots distributed across 6 orbital planes which ensure that an absolute minimum of 4 satellites are visible at any time from any place on the surface of the Earth. Other GNSS systems include GLONASS (Russia), Galileo (EU), Beidou (China), IRNSS (India) and QZSS (Japan), all in various states of operation or development (NovAtel, 2015).

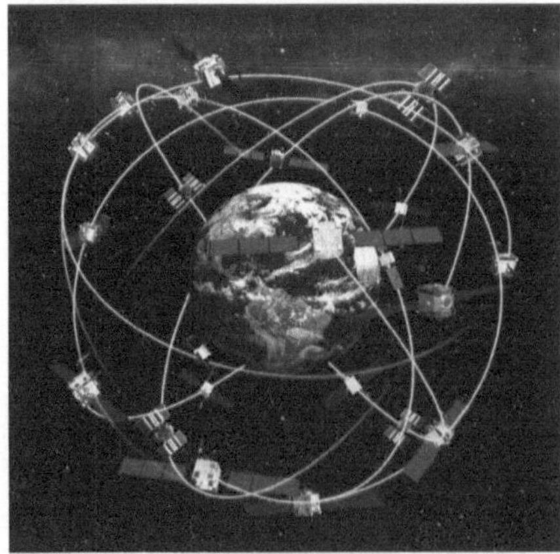

Figure 2.6: An artist's impression of the GPS satellite constellation (not to scale) in their various orbital planes around Earth (NOAA, 2018).

GPS was the first constellation of its kind and was originally called NAVSTAR. The first satellites were launched in the late 1970s and since then the constellation has undergone several generational upgrades. As of 25 August 2017, there were 31 GPS satellites in orbit of which 24 are active at all times. (NOAA, 2018). The GPS satellite constellation has an inclination of 55°and orbits the Earth at an altitude of 20200 km. The GPS satellites primarily transmit radio signals down to Earth through the ionosphere, initially for military applications and, from 1983, for general civilian use.

Each GPS satellite is identified by a Pseudo Random Noise (PRN) code in the range 1–32. Included in the continual transmissions from the satellites are ranging signals, satellite status, orbit parameters (ephemerides), and a Space Vehicle Number (SVN) (in addition to the PRN).

Receivers on the ground use the signal travel time to determine their range from each satellite and use ionospheric TEC models to make corrections to the estimated range. Since the orbital parameters of the satellites are precisely known, GPS receivers can use a method called trilateration to determine their current position and speed (Yuen et al., 2009).

The travel time for each GPS satellite signal to reach the receiver can be calculated using the transmission time data embedded within the signal itself and the time of reception. Radio waves propagate at the speed of light (in a vacuum) and so the pseudorange between the receiver and the satellite can easily be calculated. A variety of atmospheric, ionospheric and geometric factors can produce a slight decrease in the signal speed. A 1 μs delay can result in a 300 m error in the range calculation.

Three GNSS satellites are required in order to calculate the location of the receiver as shown in Figure 2.7. A fourth GNSS satellite is required to calculate the timing correction, as the intersection of the first three range spheres results in two potential locations. The fourth satellite identifies the actual location. If more GNSS satellite signals are available to use in the location calculation, the final position estimate becomes more accurate.

The primary operating frequency (L1) of GPS is 1575.42 MHz. Despite the high frequency, the ionosphere can cause retardation of radio waves which result in worst-case range errors on the order of 100 m. A secondary operating frequency (L2) running at 1227.60 MHz was introduced to the GPS system. It is referred to as "L2C" where the C stands for "civilian" (NOAA, 2018). This allowed for the automatic correction of rate and range errors which compensates for the effect of the ionosphere on position estimates. Because the ionosphere is dispersive, signals of different frequencies travel at different velocities. The receiver determines the ionospheric time delay from the differences in arrival time of the two frequencies.

Completed in February 2016, the newest Block (IIF) of GPS satellites have an additional available band, L5 (1176.45 MHz), which is specifically intended for aeronautical radio-navigation applications. Additional frequencies allow for multiple estimates of the ionospheric delay in order to reduce the position error. Despite an improved design which provides higher accuracy, it has been shown that high-latitude scintillations have a greater effect on L5 and L2 than on L1 signals (Peng and Morton, 2011). This research does not make use of the L5 signals.

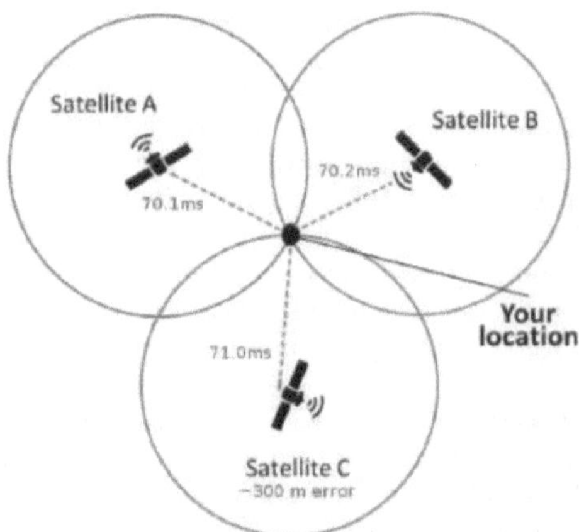

Figure 2.7: Trilateration is a technique used by GPS receivers to determine their exact spatial location on a flat plane (2 dimensions) by determining the intersection point of three overlapping range circles with known radii. In 3 dimensions, the intersections are from three overlapping range spheres, instead of circles, resulting in two potential locations. A fourth satellite (not pictured) is required to determine which of the two locations is the correct one.

By using two frequencies, the actual TEC values can be derived and may result in a 50% RMS correction to the ionospheric time delay (Klobuchar, 1987). These values can then be applied to single-frequency receivers to perform error correction as discussed in Section 2.4.

A fourth civilian frequency, "L1C", is expected to be included in the future Block III generation of GPS satellites. This additional frequency will allow for greater interoperability with the EU's Galileo system, and will serve as the interoperability standard as Japan, India and China intend to also broadcast L1C. Upgrades to the GPS system are also expected to include new additional military frequencies for use by the US (NovAtel, 2015).

2.5.2   GPS Lock Time

Lock time is a continuous count from the time since a unique PRN signal is acquired until the signal is lost. A graph of the lock time should present as a continuous linear increase. By overlaying this with a satellite's visibility (see section 2.5.5), it is easy to determine if a loss of lock occurred during a satellite's visible time as the lock time value would drop back to zero and the count begins anew. Separate lock time counts are recorded for different frequencies.

When loss of lock occurs on all visible satellites simultaneously, this is indicative of a physical issue affecting the receiver (such as a loss of power) rather than interruption of the signal from the satellites. Because of the scale size and drift velocities of the ionospheric irregularities, it is statistically unlikely that scintillation would occur over the entire sky simultaneously. Locked GPS satellites tend to be scattered throughout the sky at any given time; this is an intentional design of the GPS constellation, as trilateration becomes more accurate with a greater distribution of ray paths (see section 2.5.6). A schematic of the varying effect of scintillation structures on GPS satellites as they spread across the visible sky is shown in Figure 2.8.

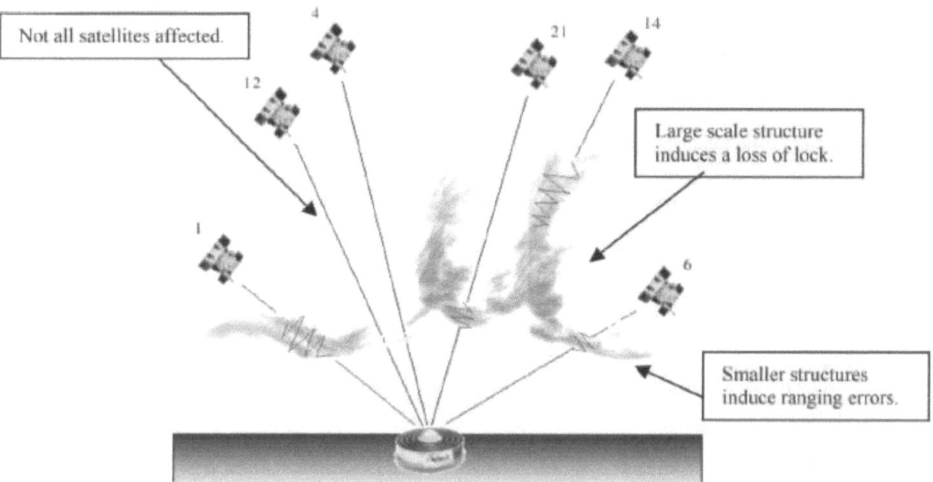

Figure 2.8: A schematic of the types of scintillation structures in the ionosphere and their varying effect on satellite signals (SBAS Ionospheric Working Group, 2010)

Loss of lock does not threaten the integrity of the signal, merely the availability, but it reduces the redundancy and may affect the accuracy of the position estimate. It is a useful first-line indicator of any potential interference with the signal, or problems with the receiver.

2.5.3 Carrier-to-Noise-Density Ratio (C/N_o)

The strength of the signal from the GPS satellites can be indicated in a variety of ways. The most commonly used methods are Signal-to-Noise Ratio (SNR) and Carrier-to-Noise-Density Ratio (C/N_o). These two terms are often used interchangeably, but have significant fundamental differences (Badke, 2009; Damm, 2010).

The SNR is a ratio, measured in decibels (dB), which describes the ratio of signal power (S) to noise power (N) within a given bandwidth. It is an expression of *"the amount by which a signal level exceeds its corresponding noise"* (Freeman, 1981). SNR is a measurement applied to a baseband signal. C/N_o is also a ratio, usually expressed in decibel-Hertz (dB-Hz), which describes the ratio of the carrier power to the noise power *per unit bandwidth*.

C/N_o is thus a carrier-to-noise-power-spectral-*density* ratio. C/N_o is often used to characterise impairments in a network as it is applied to raw Radio Frequency (RF) signals. In this case, the raw RF signal is the carrier wave of the GPS satellite signal. Typical C/N_o values for an L1 receiver are between 37 to 45 db-Hz (Joseph, 2010).

C/N_o should not be confused with the Carrier-to-Noise Ratio (C/N). To calculate C/N_o requires the carrier power C and the noise power spectral density N_o. N_o is the amount of noise power (measured in watts) per unit of bandwidth (in Hz). The total signal power S (in watts) is often taken as equivalent to the unmodulated carrier power C (at entry to the receiver). The widely accepted formulas for SNR (in dB) and C/N_o (in db-Hz) are:

$$SNR = 10log_{10}\left(\frac{S_{rms}}{N_{rms}}\right) \tag{2.8}$$

$$C/N_o = 10log_{10}\left(\frac{C}{N_o}\right) \tag{2.9}$$

The C/N_o values used in this research were automatically calculated by the GISTM receiver software and written to the data file. Since amplitude scintillation (S_4) can be identified through short-duration deep fades in the C/N_o these values were used as another indicator of scintillation events. C/N_o has additional practical uses in GNSS. When comparing the capabilities of different GNSS receivers, C/N_o is a far more useful metric than SNR because the receiver bandwidth is eliminated from the comparison.

SNR alone can be misleading as a specific receiver may have a good SNR, but once the device's bandwidth is factored in then the C/N_o may be significantly higher (Badke, 2009). If the noise bandwidth (NBW) of the specific receiver's SNR measurement is known then the C/N_o can be derived from SNR through the relation:

$$\frac{C}{N_o} = SNR + 10log_{10}\left(\frac{2 \cdot NBW}{f_s \cdot \tau}\right) \tag{2.10}$$

In this relation, the sampling frequency is f_s (samples per second) and τ is the accumulation period (in seconds).

2.5.4 Multipath and Multipath Errors

Multipath is a type of error which occurs when a direct signal from a GNSS satellite is combined with a reflected signal off a nearby object before being received by the antenna. The reflected ray path travels a longer distance, inducing a delay in the signal travel time which results in the incorrect estimation of the receiver location. Multipath errors can be caused by the ground, bodies of water, trees, buildings or nearby mountains. When multipath errors occur in developed urban areas, the effect is often referred to as 'urban canyoning'.

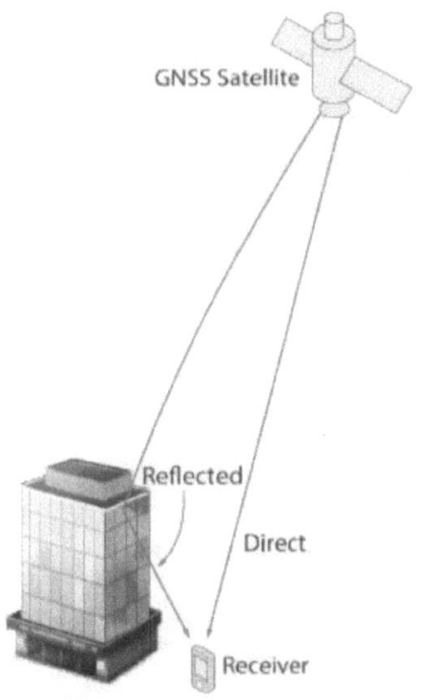

Figure 2.9: A diagram showing the concept of multipath errors: GNSS signals may be reflected off a surface such as a building before reaching the receiver (Image amended from NovAtel, 2015).

If the receiver is not stationary then reflected signals tend to fail to converge on the target antenna and only signals which have been directly received are used (Atilaw et al., 2015). Many GNSS receivers are programmed to ignore extreme outliers that result from long multipath delays. Short-delay multipath signals may have different frequencies or lower power and can be mitigated through the use of special antennas or by frequency analysis (Yuen et al., 2009).

The easiest method to reduce the risk of multipath errors is to ensure that the GNSS antenna is clear of nearby obstructions or reflective surfaces. If removing all potential nearby obstructions is not possible, a fixed elevation mask or an azimuth-dependent elevation mask appropriate to the environment can be used to discard data from signals below a certain threshold (Atilaw et al., 2015).

In the case of the SA Agulhas II at sea, it is expected that the only potential source of multipath errors is the ocean surface. There are no mountains, trees or any other geographic obstructions projecting above the ocean horizon which may cause multipath errors or block line of sight to a satellite. The antenna is elevated above sea level as well as the superstructure of the ship (see Figure 3.2(b) for more detail). It is expected that this will provide a clear horizon-to-horizon view for the GISTM antenna.

2.5.5 Theoretical Visibility of GPS Satellites

The visibility of GPS satellites (by the receiver) is an important factor for this research. Obstructions in the line of sight between the receiver and the satellite reduce the period in which the receiver can lock onto the satellite signal.

When a satellite is near the horizon, the signals to the receiver travel a much longer distance through the atmosphere and the ionosphere than when the satellite is at zenith. This increases the likelihood of signal retardation and disruption, so signals originating from low elevations are discarded, leaving only stronger, better connections to higher-elevation satellites.

Low-elevation signals also have a higher risk of being subject to multipath errors. The generally accepted elevation cut-off to reduce these potential errors is 10° (Cilliers et al., 2006; Trimble, 2018; Van Dierendonck, 2009), however it is at the discretion of the researcher to determine the best elevation mask for their specific antenna environment. Some use 15° (SBAS Ionospheric Working Group, 2010) while others go as high as 20° (Carrano et al., 2005).

To predict the visibility of GNSS satellites from any location on Earth at any given time, a free web-based software package called Trimble can be used. Trimble provides options for modelling not only satellite availability, but also TEC maps, scintillation maps, and ionospheric index. Trimble allows the user to select which GNSS constellations to include, and to specify the elevation of the simulated receiver, as well as the elevation cutoff (Trimble, 2018).

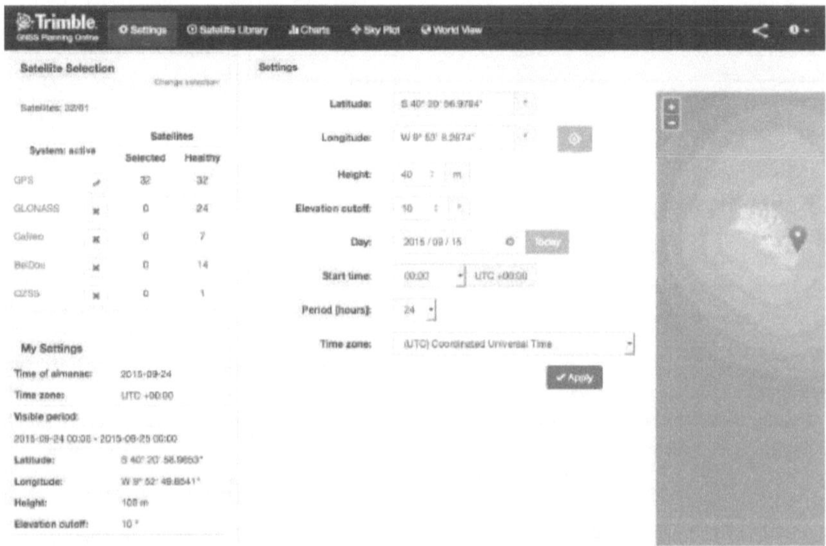

Figure 2.10: The Trimble web interface (Trimble, 2018).

The Trimble software was used to obtain the theoretical satellite visibility and elevation maps (see Figure 2.11) using only the GPS constellation (PRN 1–32), for 15 September 2015 from Gough Island, in order to best model the expected output of the data from the GISTM located there. A 10° elevation mask was used as per industry norm.

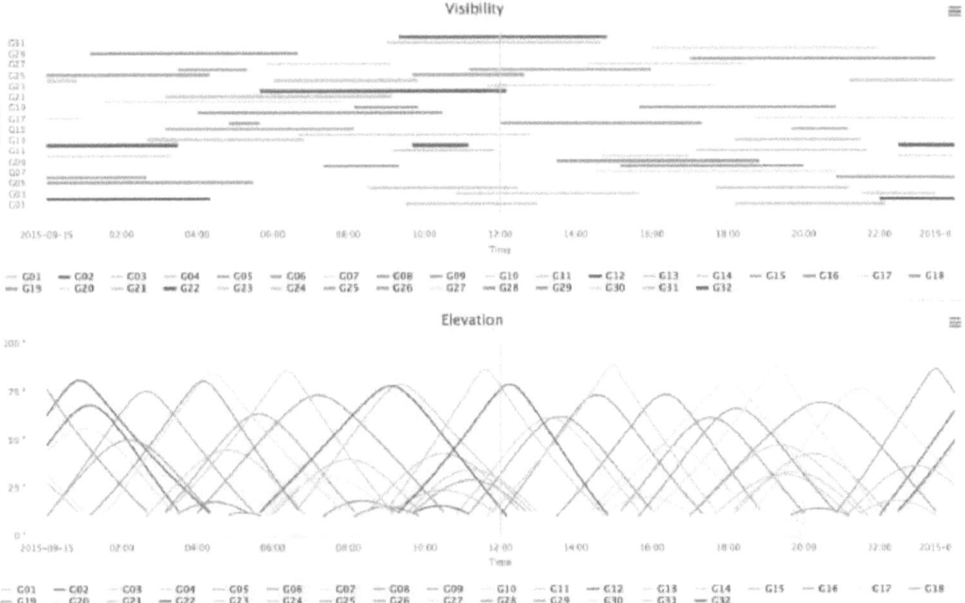

Figure 2.11: (Top): The theoretical visibility periods of the GPS satellites. (Bottom): The theoretical elevation map of the GPS satellites. Both were modelled using Trimble, as seen from Gough Island on 15 September 2015 (Trimble, 2018).

The results showed a fairly well-balanced distribution of satellite elevations and coverage throughout the entire day. This is not unexpected, as the general design of the GPS constellation is to provide continuous coverage by multiple satellites at all times for almost anywhere on Earth.

Using Trimble, several satellites were predicted to drop below the 10°elevation limit in rapid succession at 13:00 on 15 September 2015; coverage decreased to only 5 satellites. Trimble can be used to draw maps for 8 years prior to the current date and up to 3 months in advance, and the duration to be mapped can be either 6, 12 or 24 hours.

2.5.6 Dilution Of Precision (DOP)

Another potential source of positioning errors in GPS is the physical geometric arrangement of the satellites throughout the sky. When the satellites are clustered together, the angles between the receiver and the incident ray paths are too small to perform accurate trilateration as the uncertainty in the intersection points between the pseudoranges is increased. When satellites have a good angular separation, the location of the receiver has greater certainty.

The degree to which the current geometric spread of satellites affects the position accuracy is measured through Dilution of Precision (DOP). DOP is a measure of geometric strength (Yuen et al., 2009) and is defined as *"a numerical representation of satellite geometry... dependent on the locations of satellites that are visible to the receiver"* (NovAtel, 2015). The lower the DOP value is, the more accurate the position calculation will be. The DOP can be used to intelligently select satellites for use in a position estimate by identifying which satellites cause the greatest degradation in the accuracy of the calculation and ignoring those signals to minimise the DOP.

(a) (b)

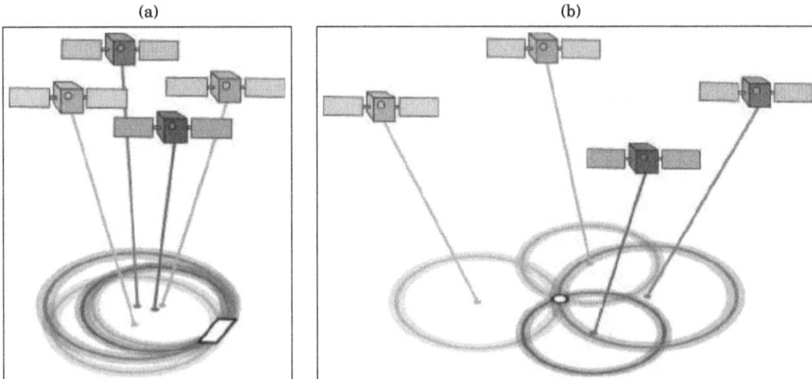

Figure 2.12: Two graphics showing different angular separation geometry for a group of GPS satellites in orbit above a receiver. (a) High DOP: When GPS satellites are clustered together, the angular separation between the incoming ray paths is low, resulting in less accurate position estimates. (b) Low DOP: When the GPS satellites are spread out, the angular separation is high, and the position estimate is more accurate (Beary, 2014).

The number of visible satellites has a direct influence on the DOP. The more satellites available to use, the greater the likelihood of obtaining a selection of 4 satellites with a good geometric distribution. The ideal 4-satellite geometry for a highly accurate position estimate is a tetrahedron, with three visible satellites distributed equi-angularly around the receiver location, just above the receiver's horizon (or the selected elevation cutoff), and for the fourth visible satellite to be directly overhead or close to zenith with respect to the receiver. The volume of the tetrahedron is inversely correlated with the DOP. The greater the tetrahedron's volume, the lower the DOP value becomes (Langley, 1999).

DOP as a measure can be broken down into several components. In general, the value used for the interpretation of DOP is called Geometric Dilution of Precision (GDOP). It describes the combined overall accuracy of the 3D Position and Time. Other aspects of DOP are:

- PDOP (Position): the accuracy of the 3D position (X,Y,Z), also known as spherical DOP.
- TDOP (Time): the accuracy of the satellite's atomic clock.
- VDOP (Vertical): the accuracy of the 1D height position (Z).
- HDOP (Horizontal): the accuracy of the 2D Latitude & Longitude position (X,Y).

GDOP is a complex combination of error measurements, vector matrix algebra, and receiver position estimate variances: σ_E^2, σ_N^2, and σ_U^2 are the variances from the East, North, and Up components of the receiver position estimate. σ_T^2 is the variance of the clock offset estimate of the receiver. The receiver-satellite geometry can be represented through the trace elements of a matrix $\boldsymbol{D}$. σ is the standard deviation of the User Equivalent Range Error (UERE). The equations to relate these terms to each other are as follows (Langley, 1999):

$$\sigma_G = \sqrt{\sigma_T^2 + \sigma_U^2 + \sigma_N^2 + \sigma_E^2} \tag{2.11}$$

$$= \sigma \cdot \sqrt{D_{44} + D_{33} + D_{22} + D_{11}} \tag{2.12}$$

where

$$GDOP = \sqrt{D_{44} + D_{33} + D_{22} + D_{11}} \tag{2.13}$$

The various DOPs listed above can also be calculated using the East, North, Up and Time variances, or the appropriate trace elements of the geometric matrix $\boldsymbol{D}$. The formulas are:

$$PDOP = \frac{\sigma_P}{\sigma} = \sqrt{D_{33} + D_{22} + D_{11}} \quad \text{where} \quad \sigma_P = \sqrt{\sigma_U^2 + \sigma_N^2 + \sigma_E^2} \tag{2.14}$$

$$HDOP = \frac{\sigma_H}{\sigma} = \sqrt{D_{22} + D_{11}} \quad \text{where} \quad \sigma_H = \sqrt{\sigma_N^2 + \sigma_E^2} \tag{2.15}$$

$$VDOP = \frac{\sigma_U}{\sigma} = \sqrt{D_{33}} \quad \text{where} \quad \sigma_U = \sqrt{\sigma_U^2} \tag{2.16}$$

$$VDOP = \frac{\sigma_T}{\sigma} = \sqrt{D_{44}} \quad \text{where} \quad \sigma_T = \sqrt{\sigma_T^2} \tag{2.17}$$

The various aspects of DOP are interrelated as well, with $PDOP^2 = HDOP^2 + VDOP^2$ as well as $GDOP^2 = PDOP^2 + TDOP^2$ (Langley, 1999).

If the location of the receiver is known (or can be estimated), it is possible to predict DOP values for any future date by using a GPS satellite almanac. Such an almanac provides the ephemeris and time information, including clock adjustments for leap seconds (Yuen et al., 2009).

The Trimble software also contains this capability, allowing the expected number of visible satellites and thus also the predicted GDOP to be modelled as seen in Figure 2.13. The drop in the number of satellites at approximately 13:00 is clearly visible, as is the related increase in the GDOP, both of which are congruent with the visibility map in Figure 2.11.

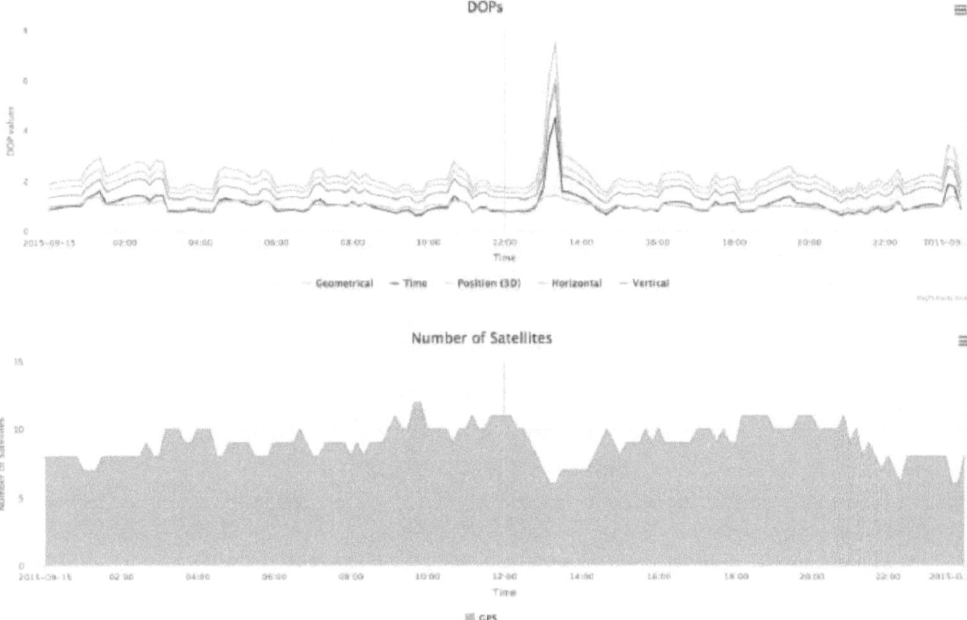

Figure 2.13: Top (a): The expected DOP for GPS as seen from Gough Island on 15
September 2015 calculated using Trimble. A significant increase in DOP occurs at
approximately 13:00 local time. Below (b): The predicted number of GPS satellites
for the same location and time. The increase in DOP in (a) is congruent with a sharp
decline in the number of visible GPS satellites at the same time (Trimble, 2018).

DOP is an important factor to consider when assessing the accuracy of a position estimate. If any
irregularities in the GPS signal are observed, it would be beneficial to determine the associated DOP in
the attempt to determine the cause.

2.5.7   Other sources of GPS errors

There are a number of other well-understood potential sources of errors for GNSS that should be kept in
mind when determining the accuracy of position estimates. Modern GNSS implementations compensate
for these errors where possible. They vary from intentional denial of service and intentionally introduced
errors, to satellite-side errors and receiver-side errors, and are listed in this general order in the brief
descriptions below.

Jamming

By the time GPS signals have travelled the 20200 km from the satellite in orbit to reach the receiver on the ground they have been significantly weakened. Other strong sources of Electromagnetic (EM) radiation which may be nearby the receiver can overpower the signal from the satellite, preventing the receiver from acquiring a lock. When done intentionally it is referred to as Jamming (NovAtel, 2015). Natural jamming can also occur when a solar flare produces strong EM radiation. It can also occur in the SAMA during a geomagnetic storm when the influence of the Van Allen Radiation Belt is strongest (Yuen et al., 2009).

Spoofing

Spoofing is an intentional form of GNSS denial where a signal generator is used to introduce a false signal and altered message, thereby tricking the receiver into calculating incorrect pseudoranges. Spoofing can be overcome by tracking an encrypted signal from the GNSS constellation in use, if access is available to the encrypted channels. A receiver that can track more than one frequency or more than one constellation can also detect and overcome spoofing, as the complexity and sophistication levels of the hardware and software required increase when more than one signal or constellation has to be spoofed simultaneously (NovAtel, 2015).

Selective Availability

When GPS was originally built it was intended only for use by the US military. In 1983 a commercial airliner was shot down after accidentally flying into restricted USSR airspace, resulting in the deaths of 269 people. This tragedy could have been prevented by basic access to GPS, and so it was made freely available for civilian use in the interest of the common good (Jewell, 2007).

In order to retain military positioning superiority as a matter of national security, intentional degradation through satellite clock dithering and ephemerides manipulation was implemented in the public signals to produce position errors of up to 100 m. Over time the civilian market developed new techniques, such as differential GPS, which could counteract Selective Availability.

On 1 May 2000 the US government turned off Selective Availability, and civilian positioning accuracy improved dramatically. However, the option to reactivate it remained and civilian users worldwide operated under this uncertainty. In 2007 the US Government declared that it had no intention of reinstating Selective Availability, and future GPS satellites would not have this capability (GPSWorld, 2007; Hofmann-Wellenhof et al., 2001).

Atomic Clock Error

The Cesium and/or Rubidium atomic clocks used in the GPS satellites are precise to the nanosecond. However, the clocks can encounter noise and drift errors, and may not be exactly synchronised to the true time. These minute deviations (up to 10 nanoseconds) can cause up to 3 m position offsets (Hofmann-Wellenhof et al., 2001; NovAtel, 2015).

Ephemeris

The information contained in the signal from a GPS satellite includes the ephemeris (orbital parameters) of that particular space vehicle. This broadcast message is repeated with high regularity, but the information in the message can be several hours old. The orbits of GPS satellites are fairly stable and well-known, so deviations from the expected location are very small. These orbital inaccuracies cause around 2.5 m position errors (Klobuchar, 1987; NovAtel, 2015).

Relativity

GPS satellites have a very high orbital velocity because of their altitude. The theory of special relativity posits that fast-moving objects experience time dilation. The closer an object comes to the speed of light, the greater the time dilation factor becomes, and the more time slows down for the moving object. However, general relativity predicts that the weaker the gravitational potential experienced by an object, the faster time moves for that object.

The Earth's gravitational field strength at a distance of 20200 km is weaker than that at the Earth's surface, but not enough to counteract the velocity time dilation effect. The clock on the GPS satellite will thus tick slower than a clock on Earth. These discrepancies have been precisely measured, and the clock on board a GPS satellite is thus adjusted before launch in order to run at the correct rate once in orbit (Hofmann-Wellenhof et al., 2001).

Sagnac Distortion

GPS signal travel time is defined according to an inertial reference frame. Observations of signal travel time are processed using an Earth-centred Earth-fixed (ECEF) frame. A Lorentz transformation is used for the conversion between the inertial reference frame and the ECEF frame. The algebraic sign of the correction depends on whether the satellite is in the eastern or western celestial hemisphere. Neglecting to use the right algebraic sign produces an east-west error on the scale of tens of meters (Hofmann-Wellenhof et al., 2001).

Biases and Noise

The pseudoranges calculated between a receiver and a specific satellite can be affected by both satellite bias and receiver bias, as well as built-in noise within either of those systems. The satellite bias can be calculated by differencing between multiple receivers, while the receiver bias can be determined by differencing between multiple satellites (Hofmann-Wellenhof et al., 2001). The system noise values can usually be determined through testing before the receiver is sold, or the satellite is launched.

2.6   The SA Agulhas II

The SA Agulhas II (pictured in Figure 2.14) is a state-of-the-art South African ice-breaking resupply and research vessel dedicated to the southern oceans and the Antarctic. Commissioned in 2012, it carries 45 crew and 100 scientists and supports a variety of oceanographic, environmental, climate, ice, vibration and space science activities. The GISTM antenna used in this research is installed at the top of the main mast of the ship. The hardware, as well as technical matters related to the SA Agulhas II, are discussed in greater detail in Chapter 3.

Figure 2.14: A photograph of the SA Agulhas II approaching the Akta Bukta ice shelf in Antarctica, on 6 February 2015 (Vermeulen et al., 2016).

The SA Agulhas II undertakes three major voyages each year: to Marion Island in April and May, to Gough Island in September and October, and to Antarctica (with a stop at South Georgia) from December to February. The Antarctic voyage occasionally includes stops at Bouvet Island. A number of shorter voyages in the oceans around South Africa are performed for educational purposes in between the major journeys (SA Dep. of Environmental Affairs, 2018). A location track map of the SA Agulhas II over a 3-year period (2013, 2014 and 2015) is shown in Figure 2.15.

The SA Agulhas II was built in Finland by STX and first launched to sea on 21 July 2011. It is dedicated to the memory of South African icon, singer, democracy stalwart, and education advocate Miriam Makeba. The SA Agulhas II is licensed to transport passengers, food, supplies, vehicles, helicopters as well as flammable fuels.

It also houses eight dedicated research laboratories as well as space for six containerised laboratories on the aft deck. Modern and fully-featured, it has a hospital, library, gym, sauna, laundry, auditorium,

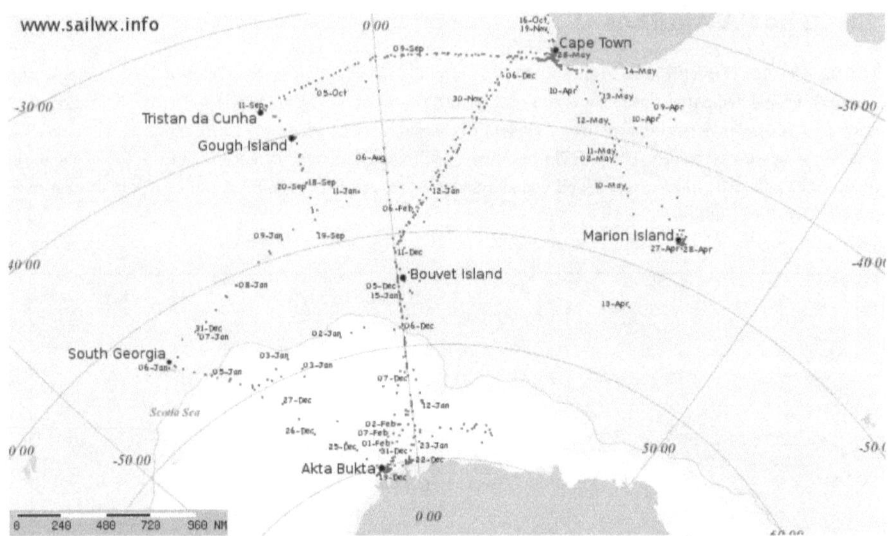

Figure 2.15: The route of the SA Agulhas II through the Southern Ocean in 2013-2015 to Antarctica, Gough Island, South Georgia and Tristan da Cunha, as well as Marion Island (Amended from Sailwx, 2015).

business centre, gear locker, dining hall, and two lounges for passengers.

2.7 Gough Island

Gough Island, shown in Figure 2.16, is a dependency of the British overseas territory of St Helena and is located at 40.345°S, 9.880°W, (40°20' 58.90" S, 9°52' 49.35" W) in the South Atlantic Ocean. It was formerly known as Diego Alvarez, and is a 91 km^2 volcanic island with a maximum height of 910 m above sea level. It is 2700 km from Cape Town.

The meteorological station on the island is occupied year-round by 6-8 South Africans (SA Dep. of Environmental Affairs, 2018) employed by the South African National Antarctic Program (SANAP), a division of the Department of Environmental Affairs (DEA). The station hosts a GISTM identical to the one aboard the SA Agulhas II, the location of which is marked with a red dot in the inset of Figure 2.16.

SANSA also operates GISTM units on Marion Island, in Hermanus, South Africa, and at the SANAE-IV station in Antarctica. As the only fixed station located within the SAMA, the Gough Island GISTM was the only source of scintillation data for this area of interest. The majority of the SAMA lies beyond the coverage of these few fixed stations as shown in Figure 2.17. The maximum theoretical coverage range of a dual-frequency GISTM such as the one used in this research was calculated using a 300 km Ionospheric Pierce Point (IPP) height.

2.8 Ionospheric Pierce Points (IPP)

The Ionospheric Pierce Point (IPP) is part of a TEC calculation method in which it is assumed that the ionosphere is a single thin shell and that the ray paths of the signals from the satellites will pierce the ionosphere at that particular altitude as illustrated in Figure 2.18. The IPP altitudes used in associated research vary from 300 km (Cilliers et al., 2006) and 350 km (Habarulema et al., 2009; Kintner et al., 2007) to 400 km (van der Merwe, 2011) depending on the ionospheric shell model being used.

The theoretical IPP range of GPS coverage is calculated using a 10° elevation cut-off (Cilliers et al., 2006). The IPP radius (R_{IPP}) is a function of satellite elevation angle (E) and the selected IPP height (H) and is calculated as follows:

$$z = (90 - E) \tag{2.18}$$

$$z' = \frac{\arcsin(R_e \cdot \sin(z \cdot \pi/180))}{R_e + H} \tag{2.19}$$

$$R_{IPP} = R_e \cdot \pi/180 \cdot (z - z') \tag{2.20}$$

R_e is the mean radius of the Earth (6378.1370 km). The graph shown in Figure 2.19 illustrates the relationship between R_{IPP} and E (MATLAB code authored by B. Opperman & P. Cilliers, pers. comm. 28 Sep 2018) for a chosen IPP height of 300 km. The lower the satellite elevation angle becomes, the wider the IPP radius will be.

Figure 2.16: A topographical map of Gough Island with satellite imagery insert showing the location of the GISTM antenna at the South African research station on the South-Eastern edge of the island (Image amended from Google Earth, 2017; Wikimedia Commons, 2007).

2.9   Geomagnetic storms and SYM-H

During strong geomagnetic storms, high-energy particle precipitation increases. This results in the electron concentration of the ionosphere being disturbed, which causes the development of high-density patches and low-density bubbles. When an electromagnetic wave such as a GPS radio signal encounters the edges of these structures, the rapid variation in electron density scatters the radio waves and causes ionospheric scintillation (Doherty et al., 2003).

The Disturbance storm time (Dst) index is often used as a high temporal resolution version (in nT) of the K-index, which is an indicator of geomagnetic storms on a global level. The K-index is 3-hourly, while Dst provides hourly indicators for geomagnetic storm conditions. The greatest difference between Symmetric-Horizontal disturbance index (SYM-H) and Dst is time resolution.

The 1-min SYM-H index (in nT) is an even higher temporal resolution indicator of geomagnetic storm state than Dst. SYM-H is calculated using a six-station average of the symmetric portion of the horizontal

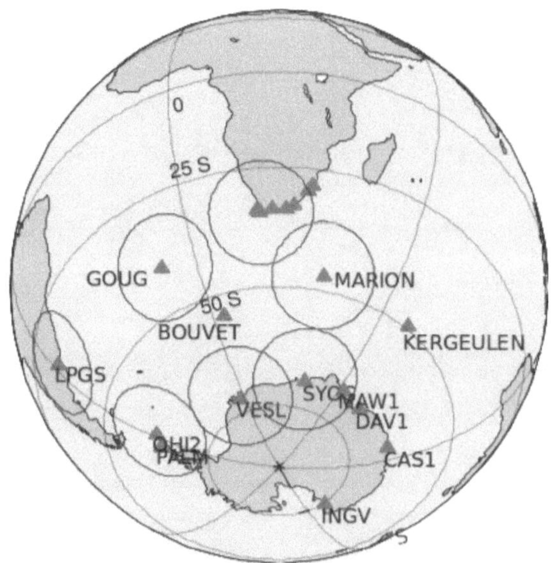

Figure 2.17: The theoretical coverage range (R_{IPP}) of the stationary GISTMs in the Southern Oceans using a 300 km IPP altitude (Cilliers et al., 2006).

component of the magnetic field near the equator, which is then corrected for latitude.

The high resolution SYM-H has a greater ability to show magnetic field variations resulting from storm conditions. A moderate geomagnetic storm measures between -50 nT to -100 nT. An intense geomagnetic storm has values below -100 nT (Wanliss and Showalter, 2006).

The SYM-H index was checked during this research to identify the presence of any geomagnetic storms which may have adversely affected the ionosphere at the time of scintillation. The SYM-H graphs and data were sourced from the Kyoto Geomagnetic WDC (Kyoto Geomagnetic World Data Centre, 2015).

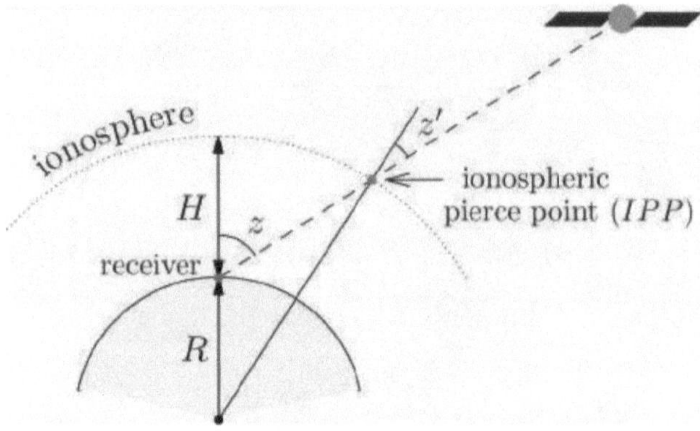

Figure 2.18: Schematic illustrating the geometry of the Ionospheric Pierce Point (Kirienko, 2007).

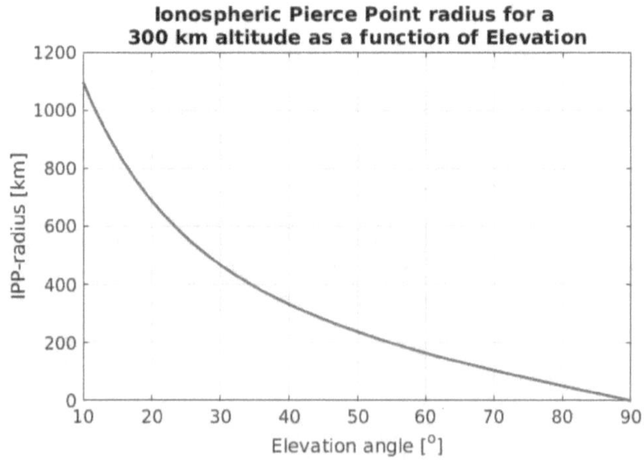

Figure 2.19: The relationship between the IPP radius and the satellite elevation angle for a chosen IPP height of 300 km.

DATA ACQUISITION

This chapter focuses on the acquisition of the data for this research. It discusses the periods in which recording took place. It details the physical hardware and software used to record the data, the format and content of the resulting data files, the conversion processes needed to render these data in an accessible format, and the error corrections which had to be employed to render the data usable for processing. A test was also performed to determine the physical tolerances of the data-gathering environment to the introduction of errors.

3.1 Availability of Data

The data made available by SANSA for this research was recorded using hardware installed on the SA Agulhas II, and consists of a total of 18 months of data recorded between mid-2014 and early 2016. During this time, the ship made four voyages through the SAMA, twice to Antarctica and twice to Gough Island.

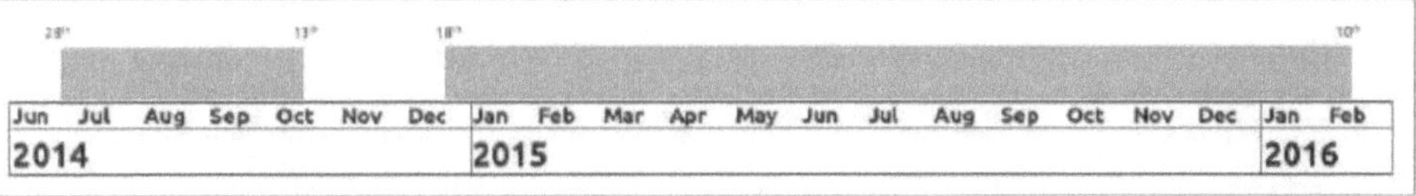

Figure 3.1: A graphic showing the periods during which data was recorded by the receiver aboard the SA Agulhas II. Four months' worth was recorded in 2014, and then a full Antarctica-Gough-Marion-Antarctica cycle was recorded over 14 uninterrupted months, including the entire 2015.

The SA Agulhas II was met at the dock in Cape Town in February of 2016 upon its return from Antarctica to retrieve the most recent scintillation data files recorded up to that time. This study was the first to access and assess this unique SAMA-traversing data set.

3.2 Hardware: NovAtel GISTM and Antenna

The GSV4004B GPS Ionospheric Scintillation and Total Electron Content Monitor (GISTM) system used in this research was developed by GPS Silicon Valley (GSV) and consists of a NovAtel EuroPak-3M GPS receiver, a power supply unit, and an antenna.

The antenna mounted aboard the SA Agulhas II is an Ashtech Choke Ring (Model GG) L1/L2 antenna protected by a semi-hemispheric radome. The purpose of the choke ring is to redirect, block, and absorb low-elevation and altered-frequency signals as these are likely to have been reflected. This is one example of using specialised antenna hardware to mitigate multipath errors.

(a)   (b)

Figure 3.2: (a): The L1/L2 Model GG Choke Ring antenna of the GISTM is mounted on the truss structure of the Crow's Nest aboard the SA Agulhas II; (b): The Crow's Nest of the SA Agulhas II. The truss above it is the highest point on the ship, and houses several instruments, including the radar.

The antenna and the receiver form the sensor component of the GISTM. The receiver passes the raw and detrended signal information from the visible GPS satellites into an external logger. The logger records the ionospheric scintillation and TEC data into data files. The logger software is discussed in Section 3.4.1.

Detrending is often done using a 6th-order Butterworth low-pass (amplitude) or high-pass (phase) filter, with a cut-off frequency specified by the user during set-up. For this research, the cut-off frequency was set to 0 Hz. As a result, the amplitude scintillation measurements were normalised by the firmware using an average over a 60 s period instead of using a Butterworth filter (Van Dierendonck, 2009).

Not using a low-pass filter can be advantageous, as research has shown that the cut-off frequency used for detrending should not be the same for all latitudes. This is because the relative drift velocities of ionospheric irregularities vary by latitude, and thus the Fresnel frequencies are also different. At high

37

latitudes, the Fresnel frequency can be an order of magnitude larger than at low latitudes. If the same cut-off frequency is used, the amplitude and phase scintillation information can be distorted (Forte and Radicella, 2002).

The EuroPak-3M GPS receiver unit (shown in Figure 3.3) consists of a Euro-3M GPS receiver board with modified firmware and a low phase noise oven-controlled crystal oscillator (OCXO) used to monitor phase scintillation, both of which are housed inside a protective enclosure.

Figure 3.3: An image of the NovAtel EuroPak-3M GPS receiver unit. Inside is a Euro-3M receiver board and a crystal oscillator (Van Dierendonck, 2009).

The Euro-3M receiver board can track up to 11 GPS signals using both the L1 (1575.42 MHz) and L2 (1227.6 MHz) frequencies. Phase and amplitude are measured at a rate of 50 Hz for each satellite being tracked on L1 (Van Dierendonck, 2009). The TEC is computed using a combination of L1 and L2 pseudorange and carrier phase measurements.

In order to measure TEC properly from a GISTM receiver, an initial receiver inter-frequency bias calculation must be performed. The bias is obtained by comparing the TEC measurements from the new unknown-bias receiver to the TEC measurements of a nearby stationary receiver with a known bias.

The receiver bias calculation was made upon initial installation of the Euro-3M on the SA Agulhas II. The inter-frequency bias was measured to be 7 TECU, with a negligible standard deviation. This bias value is comparable to the other fixed receivers in operation at that time (Cilliers et al., 2006). It is important to ensure that any studies conducted using a newly installed GISTM have performed a bias calibration before making use of the data.

3.3 The Multipath Error Roll Tolerance of the SA Agulhas II

The NovAtel GSV4004B system may be programmed (and was, in the BIOS) to exclude satellites with ray paths below 10° elevation and avoid signals reflected off nearby stationary structures. However, on a ship sailing out on the open ocean this elevation restriction may be unnecessary and would merely result in a loss of potentially valuable low-elevation scintillation data.

The SA Agulhas II is not a stationary platform. This movement factor has to be considered when identifying potential challenges to this research. The ship's motion can be described as comprising translation (travelling from point A to point B), the three axial movements (roll, pitch and yaw), and vibration (such as those generated by the engines). Of these motion sources, the side-to-side rolling motion of the ship is the most pronounced, and therefore the most likely to incur occasional multipath errors when the GISTM antenna is tilted towards the horizon.

A test was conducted to determine the antenna's physical roll angle tolerance before potentially incurring multipath errors, taking into account the buffer provided by the 10° elevation cut-off. The first step was the calculation of the horizon angle from the location of the receiver's antenna as diagrammed in Figure 3.4.

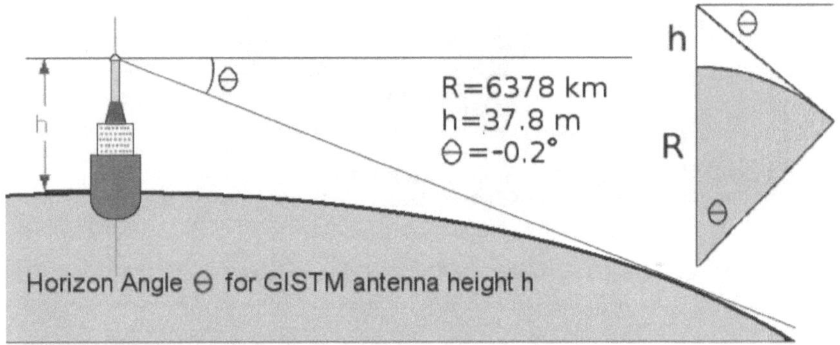

Figure 3.4: A diagram of the horizon geometry of the GISTM aboard the SA Agulhas II. A negative horizon angle of -0.2° was calculated as viewed from the position of the GISTM antenna (Vermeulen et al., 2016).

The receiver's antenna is mounted at a height (h) of 37.8 m above mean sea level and the mean radius (R) of the Earth is taken as 6378 km. This geometric calculation results in a horizon elevation angle of $\theta =$ -0.2°. The antenna-to-horizon distance was calculated to be 22.219 km.

The second step was to determine the maximum roll angle of the ship before the 10° elevation cut-off is overcome and signal reflections from the ocean surface may occur. Using the same geometry, the elevation angle to the horizon was plotted as a function of the roll angle of the ship, as shown in Figure 3.5.

Roll angles of up to 20° off vertical can be tolerated before the 10° GISTM elevation angle cut-off is breached and multipath signals could be received (Vermeulen et al., 2016). In practice, the SA Agulhas II has a maximum roll angle of 10° off vertical. Then, should the ship roll from side-to-side more than three times, an anti-roll system engages, using rapidly transferred water ballast to counteract the rolling motion of the ship for a smoother sailing experience.

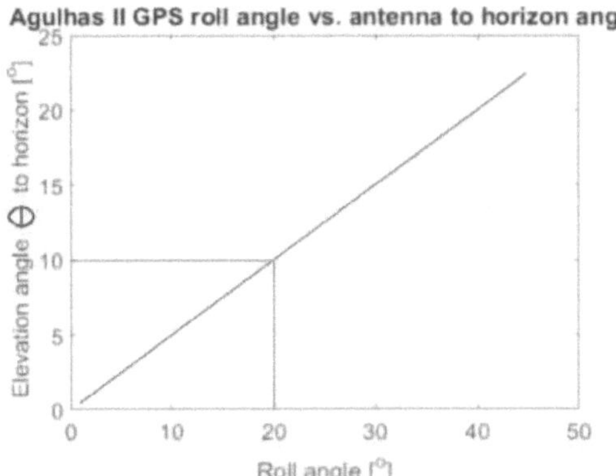

Figure 3.5: The horizon elevation angle from the GISTM antenna as a function of the roll angle of the SA Agulhas II shows a 20° roll tolerance before the 10°elevation cut-off is exceeded (Vermeulen et al., 2016).

Such extreme rolling only occurs in heavy storm conditions with large swells. Even then, it is highly unlikely that the SA Agulhas II will roll far enough off vertical for the horizon to exceed the 10° elevation cut-off and potentially incur multipath errors from the ocean surface. Additionally, the choke ring of the antenna can mitigate such multipath errors. The likelihood of the SA Agulhas II GISTM incurring multipath errors during a voyage is thus extremely low.

3.4 Data Recording Software

3.4.1 Logger Software: GPS-SCINDA

The Scintillation Network and Decision Aid (SCINDA) is a global ground-based sensor network of passive Ultra High Frequency (UHF), L-band and GPS scintillation receivers developed by the US Air Force Research Laboratory to measure scintillation, drift velocities and TEC. The SCINDA system allows for the real-time retrieval of sensor data via the Internet and is intended to support research into space weather. The GPS data logging software developed specifically for use by SCINDA is called GPS-SCINDA (Carrano and Groves, 2009).

GPS-SCINDA is a freely available, open-source package which runs in Linux. The external logging computer aboard the SA Agulhas II uses the GPS-SCINDA software. Scintillation data from the Europak-3M receiver is automatically processed in real-time by GPS-SCINDA, including the removal of outliers, the derivation of additional scintillation parameters, and the aggregation of the 50 Hz data to 1-minute parameter files.

The GPS-SCINDA software allows for thresholds to be set to determine what data is recorded and what is discarded. An example is the elevation cut-off. If set to 5° then GPS-SCINDA polls the relevant incoming data stream to determine whether the satellite elevation is above the selected threshold. If not, that particular record is discarded. The retained data is concatenated and recorded in hourly binary files. They are named in the format of 'YYMMDD_hhmmss.*' where the time indicates the starting point of the data file. These are logged into a directory structure arranged by year, month, day, and data file type. The binary file types recorded are:

- *.ism - ionospheric scintillation parameters (1 minute)
- *.msg - diagnostic messages
- *.nvd - raw 50 Hz data stream
- *.psn - receiver position (1 Hz)
- *.rng - pseudorange message
- *.scn - ionospheric statistics (1 minute)

The software setup was configured and is maintained by the SANSA Space Science engineering division. None of the scintillation data recorded during the SA Agulhas II voyages is streamed via the internet; instead it is stored locally on hard drives which are retrieved when the SA Agulhas II returns to port. The system does have Internet access, allowing SANSA engineers to connect to the system remotely to perform system tests and maintenance if needed.

Only two of the binary file types produced by GPS-SCINDA were used in this research: the *.ism file for scintillation ('ISM'), and the *.psn file for the receiver position ('PSN').

3.4.2 The ISM Binary Data File

Ionospheric Scintillation Monitor (ISM) files are saved hourly in a binary file format with the extension *.ism. They are parsed from hourly binary format using NovAtel's parseismr software, and concatenated to a daily file (Bash script: Appendix A.1.2). The output file contains 1-minute data for 28 parameters (Van Dierendonck, 2009) derived by the GISTM as shown in Table 3.1.

Only 13 of the scintillation parameters were used in this research. They are:

1.	Week	6.	L1 C/N_o	11.	TECRate 30
2.	GPSTOW	7.	S_4	12.	TEC0
3.	PRN	8.	S_{4c}	13.	L1 Lock Time
4.	Az	9.	60SecSigma		
5.	Elv	10.	TEC30		

The S_4 and σ_ϕ values in the ISM daily text file were then plotted as a histogram to test the fidelity of the data, and to test if the system is functioning correctly. Further details of the daily histogram script are available in Appendix A.1.3. The output of the daily histogram script and the subsequent data corrections are discussed in Section 3.5.

Table 3.1: The 28 scintillation parameters found in a `*.ism-derived *.txt` file.

Col	Parameter	Units/Values	Details
1	Week	1-52	Week of the year
2	GPSTOW	1-604800	Seconds of the week
3	PRN	1-32	Pseudo Random Noise Code
4	RxStatus	0 or 1	Receiver Error Status (0 = fine, 1 = error)
5	Az	degrees	Azimuth (0-360°)
6	Elv	degrees	Elevation (0-90°)
7	L1 C/N_o	db-Hz	Carrier-to-noise density ratio
8	S_4	dimensionless	Total S_4 (amplitude scintillation)
9	S_{4c}	dimensionless	Corrected S_4
10	1SecSigma	radians	σ_ϕ (phase scintillation) residuals over 1 s
11	3SecSigma	radians	σ_ϕ (phase scintillation) residuals over 3 s
12	10SecSigma	radians	σ_ϕ (phase scintillation) residuals over 10 s
13	30SecSigma	radians	σ_ϕ (phase scintillation) residuals over 30 s
14	60SecSigma	radians	σ_ϕ (phase scintillation) residuals over 60 s
15	Code-Carrier	meters	Average of Code/Carrier Divergence
16	C-CStdev	meters	STDEV of Code/Carrier Divergence
17	TEC45	TECU	TEC at TOW-45 seconds
18	TECRate45	TECU	Δ TEC from TOW-60 to TOW-45
19	TEC30	TECU	TEC at TOW-30 seconds
20	TECRate30	TECU	Δ TEC from TOW-45 to TOW-30
21	TEC15	TECU	TEC at TOW-15 seconds
22	TECRate15	TECU	Δ TEC from TOW-30 to TOW-15
23	TEC0	TECU	TEC at TOW
24	TECRate0	TECU	Δ TEC from TOW-15 to TOW
25	L1 LockTime	seconds	Count of time locked to satellite (L1)
26	ChanStatus		Channel Error status
27	L2 LockTime	seconds	Count of time locked to satellite (L2)
28	L2 C/N_o	db-Hz	Carrier-to-noise density ratio (L2)

3.4.3 The PSN Data File

The position files are also saved hourly (GPS-SCINDA starts a new file on the hour) and are presented in plain text format with a `*.psn` extension. After every 60 entries (1 per second) a timestamp is recorded on a separate line in the format 'T YY MM DD sssss' where 's' are the elapsed seconds of the day (Van Dierendonck, 2009). Only columns 1-4 of the PSN file (see Table 3.2) were used in this research, as well as the timestamp entries.

A sample of the data available in a PSN file is shown in Figure 3.6. The 'U' next to the PRN indicates that a satellite is being used in the calculation of the position estimate. A Bash script (see Appendix A.1.1) was used to concatenate the hourly PSN files into daily files for ease of use.

Table 3.2: The (up to) 17 position parameter columns of the `*.psn` files

Col	Parameter	Units/Values	Details
1	Latitude	degrees	The North-South position of the receiver
2	Longitude	degrees	The East-West position of the receiver
3	Altitude	meters	Height above average sea level
4	No of SVs		Number of Space Vehicle (SV)s tracked
5-17	PRNs		The PRN codes of the connected SVs

```
14  -33.9023311 18.4259145 36.417 08 17U 07U 11U 28U 19U 04U 30U 01U 120U 126U
15  -33.9023313 18.4259145 36.423 08 17U 07U 11U 28U 19U 04U 30U 01U 120U 126U
16  T 15 03 13 29377
17  -33.9023313 18.4259145 36.381 08 17U 07U 11U 28U 19U 04U 30U 01U 120U 126U
18  -33.9023319 18.4259138 36.471 08 17U 07U 11U 28U 19U 04U 30U 01U 120U 126U
19  -33.9023317 18.4259140 36.394 08 17U 07U 11U 28U 19U 04U 30U 01U 120U 126U
20  -33.9023315 18.4259139 36.448 08 17U 07U 11U 28U 19U 04U 30U 01U 120U 126U
21  -33.9023318 18.4259138 36.337 08 17U 07U 11U 28U 19U 04U 30U 01U 120U 126U
22  -33.9023316 18.4259142 36.399 08 17U 07U 11U 28U 19U 04U 30U 01U 120U 126U
23  -33.9023317 18.4259140 36.386 08 17U 07U 11U 28U 19U 04U 30U 01U 120U 126U
```

Figure 3.6: A sample of the data content of a PSN file. The GPS timestamp is visible in line 16, and corresponds to 13 March 2015 at 08:09:37 (UTC).

3.5 Data Problems and Corrections

Once the PSN and ISM data had been rendered into a usable format, the S_4 and σ_ϕ values in the ISM daily text file were plotted as a histogram using a Python script named `AGLS_Bins_v2.py` (see Appendix A.1.3 for additional details and sample histogram). This was intended as a test of the fidelity of the data, and subsequently provided the first indication of problems with the data. Every daily histogram plotted had data missing from 22:08 until the end of the day.

Investigation of the time stamps of the ISM data contained within the files revealed that the actual start time of each daily file was not 00:00 but rather 22:08 from the night before. Each file was thus missing the last 1 hr 52 min of data at the end of the file, and contained the last 1 hr 52 min of data from the day before at the start of the file.

A thorough analysis of all of the programming used, from the NovAtel system firmware to the daily histogram script, eventually revealed two distinct problem areas: (1) the conversions between GPSWeek & GPSTOW to Coordinated Universal Time (UTC), and (2) a timezone misalignment in the system configuration. Both of these are critical aspects of GPS time calculations.

3.5.1 GPS Epoch Corrections

Problem (1) was caused by two separate errors in the AGLS_Bins_v2.py daily histogram script.

(1A) Leap Seconds

GPS Time (GPST) is based on the atomic clock standard, whereas most normal clocks use UTC which is derived from the rotation of the Earth. GPS time does not automatically take into account leap seconds, thus GPST = UTC + leap seconds. The calculation from GPS time to UTC was outdated because the number of leap seconds had increased from 14 to 15 since the code was originally authored in June 2012.

For data recorded before 23:59:59.99 on 30 June 2015, an additional leap second (total of 16 s) had to be subtracted. For data recorded after 00:00:00 on 1 July 2015, two additional leap seconds had to be subtracted (total of 17 s). The most recent leap second took place at 23:59:59 on 31 December 2016, bringing the difference between GPST and UTC up to 18 s (IETF, 2018).

(1B) GPSWeek Epoch Correction Factor

There are several epochs to be aware of in GPST. The GPST epoch is the starting point from which GPS time is counted: 00:00:00 UTC on 6 January 1980. GPST is measured in a Week-of-the-Year (1-52) and Seconds-of-the-Week (0-604800) format. These two parameters are transmitted as independent parameters to the receiver from the GPS satellite. A 10-bit field is used for the GPSWeek value, which means that after 1024 weeks (19.69 years), the 10-bits have reached their maximum value, and so they roll over to count from 0 again.

When this roll-over occurs, it is termed a GPSWeek epoch. The GPSWeek value has to then be measured from that epoch instead of from the original GPST epoch. The first GPSWeek epoch ended on 21 August 1999. The next one will end on 6 April 2019. In order to avoid a repeat of the numerous receiver and firmware failures that took place, the modernisation of GPS included an upgrade from 10-bit to 13-bit messages for the GPSWeek field.

This equates to 8192 weeks (157.1 years) before the next roll-over will take place (Powers, 2017). This resolves the week roll-over issue for a much longer time. Owners of older receivers will still need to ensure their correction for the GPSWeek roll-over is implemented correctly to avoid date errors in their data.

Earlier versions of Python used a whole number for the epoch correction factor. Newer versions of Python support decimal values in the floating point numerical representation of time, for higher accuracy. The missing decimal portion of the GPSWeek correction factor had to be calculated.

This was done by taking 19.69 years (1024 weeks ÷ 52) and multiplying it by 365.26 (sidereal year) to get 7192.81 days, including leap days. To find the missing decimal portion with respect to seconds, we divide by 86400 (24 hrs × 60 min × 60 sec in one day) for a result of 0.0833 to be added to the correction factor. The original whole number correction factor used in the script was 719163 decimal seconds.

The new GPSWeek epoch correction factor of 719163.0833 resulted in the amount of missing ISM data changing from 1 hr 52 min up to 2 hrs exactly. Each daily ISM file actually began at 22:00 the previous evening, instead of 22:08. The missing 0.0833 was equivalent to an 8-min discrepancy in the calculation of UTC from GPST.

3.5.2   UTC and SAST Misalignment

The daily ISM data files still contained the last 2 hours of data from the night before, and were still missing the last 2 hours of data for that day. The cause was eventually identified after re-investigation of the NovAtel GSV4004B system configuration. The GPS-SCINDA logging software (which is responsible for the creation of hourly data files within daily folders) had been set to South African Standard Time (SAST) instead of UTC.

Since SAST = UTC + 2, the logger would end each daily folder at 00:00 SAST and start recording to the next day's folder when in reality the time was 22:00 UTC. Since all GPST calculations are done based on UTC, this led to the "missing" 2 hours of data being recorded to the wrong daily folder. The script, however, was using the actual data time stamps in the generation of the histogram, but the daily file contained no data from 22:00-00:00 for the day being plotted.

This problem was identified as persistent across the entire data set, affecting even the PSN files. A Ruby script, developed with the assistance of Toby Kurien, was used to "fix" the data set (see Appendix A.1.4 for details and code). The plotting script could then generate the histograms correctly, as seen in Figure 3.7. This confirmed the fidelity of the GISTM data set, as well as validating the functionality of the sequence of programs used to record, process, and fix the scintillation data from the NovAtel GSV4004B system on the SA Agulhas II.

The same processes were applied to the data from the Gough Island GISTM to ensure the fidelity of that data set. The time zones were correctly configured, and thus the Ruby script was not required. The epoch correction factor and leap seconds did require updating. The scintillation data was then ready for use in the scientific analysis.

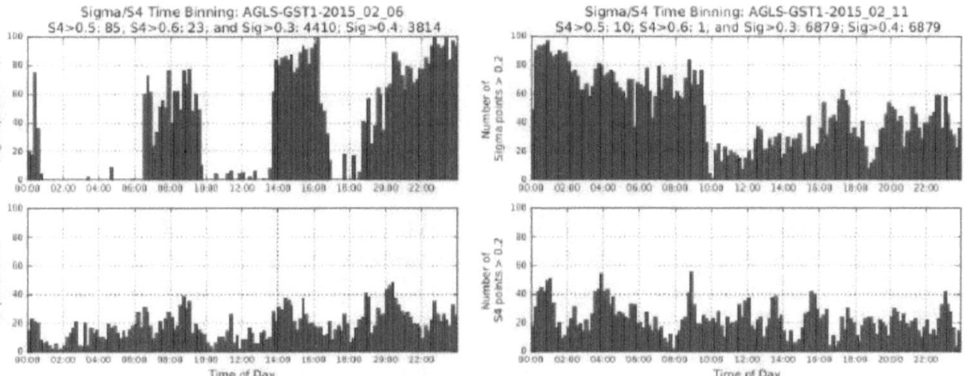

Figure 3.7: Examples of corrected daily histograms from the SA Agulhas II showing the number of S_4 and σ_ϕ values exceeding the threshold of 0.2. In the second row of the figure header are count values indicating the total number of S_4 and σ_ϕ values exceeding higher thresholds for the entire day. Counts for S_4 above 0.5 (moderate) and above 0.6 (strong) are indicated as a single value. Count values for σ_ϕ values exceeding 0.3 (moderate) and 0.4 (strong) are also shown as a single value. The purpose of the graph was to identify low-level scintillations (greater than 0.2), however, this did not provide an indication of how much higher the values were, or whether strong scintillation had occurred. Rather than re-draw every daily graph with multiple thresholds, the count values were included as a quick way to indicate how many of the reported low-level counts were, in fact, moderate or strong scintillations. The thresholds used are discussed in Section 4.1.2 and Section 4.1.3.

CHAPTER

4

I n this chapter the programs and methods used to perform the data analysis are discussed. The thresholds used to define scintillation and avoid multipath errors are shown. Examples are provided for each of the different plots which were generated using the Python and MATLAB scripts: σ_ϕ and S_4 daily histograms, 14 ISM graphs, and 10 PSN graphs.

The need for a comparison data set was identified; an assessment using geographic constraints was performed to identify the periods of intersection with the available Gough Island data. The Python and MATLAB scripts were repeated for Gough Island with modifications. The development of the running mean algorithm for position error calculation is detailed. Matching patterns or events which were observed in the graphs of differing parameters are highlighted.

4.1   Thresholds

4.1.1   Multipath error thresholds

The antenna mounted on top of the SA Agulhas II is subject to motion as the ship rolls from side to side during a voyage. It was calculated that the SA Agulhas II could roll as much as 20° off vertical before multipath errors may be incurred from signals reflecting off the ocean surface (See section 2.5.4). However, the SA Agulhas II, by design, typically does not roll more than 10° off vertical.

The choke ring of the antenna also provides physical mitigation of multipath errors from low elevation signals (see Section 3.2). Many GNSS receivers are also programmed to identify reflected signals (see Section 2.5.4) through frequency analysis in order to discard the outliers. It was thus not necessary to write any specific code for multipath error mitigation.

4.1.2 Scintillation thresholds

The strength of ionospheric scintillations are classified into four distinct categories according to the range of the dimensionless S_4 index, and the following generally-accepted terminology (Muella et al., 2014) is used to describe the intensity of a scintillation event:

- $0.2 < S_4 \leq 0.4$ - Weak
- $0.4 < S_4 \leq 0.6$ - Moderate
- $0.6 < S_4 \leq 1.0$ - Strong
- $1.0 < S_4$ - Saturated

The σ_ϕ index is measured in radians. A study of several relevant publications indicated that the choice of threshold value for σ_ϕ is generally left to the discretion of the researcher, based upon the hardware being used as well as the research objective of that particular study. In Spogli et al. (2013) the aim was to identify moderate/strong scintillations and thus a minimum threshold of 0.25 was used for both σ_ϕ (rad) and S_4.

Jiao et al. (2013) used $\sigma_\phi = 0.1$ rad (6°) and $S_4 = 0.12$ in a high-latitude study when lower threshold values were desired; for high-latitude studies which required higher threshold values, $\sigma_\phi = 0.26$ rad (15°) and $S_4 = 0.15$ were used. For this research the weak scintillation category minimum value of $S_4 = 0.2$ and a minimum σ_ϕ value of 0.2 rad (11.46°) were applied to the SA Agulhas II data.

4.1.3 Threshold values for daily scintillation count histograms

The daily scintillation count histogram script written in Python (see Section 4.2 and Appendix A.1.3 for details) made use of the following threshold values:

- Elevation cut-off: 10 (degrees) (see Section 3.3 for explanation)
- S_4 lower limit: 0.2 (only interested in seeing scintillation events)
- S_4 upper limit: 10 (selected due to noise in SA Agulhas II data, see Section 4.5)
- σ_ϕ lower limit: 0.2 (radians) (consistency with S_4)
- σ_ϕ upper limit: 10 (same as S_4 - high value due to noise)
- PRN range: 1-32 (GPS only)
- Minimum Lock Time: 240 (seconds) (recommended time for connection to stabilise)
- Number of Bins in histogram: 144 (10-minute bins)

4.1.4 Threshold values for MATLAB scintillation analysis

The following threshold values were implemented in the scintillation analysis programs written in MATLAB (see Section 4.5 and Appendix A.2):

- Elevation cut-off: 0 (degrees) (see Section 3.3 for explanation)
- S_4 lower limit: 0.05 (outlier removal and removal of 0 and NaN values)
- S_4 upper limit: 10 (selected due to noise in SA Agulhas II data, see Section 4.5.7)
- σ_ϕ lower limit: 0.05 (radians) (consistency with S_4)
- σ_ϕ upper limit: 30 (radians) (higher than S_4 - necessary due to excessive noise)
- PRN range: 1-32 (GPS only)

4.2 Daily scintillation count histograms (SA Agulhas II data)

The first data analysis undertaken was the plotting of daily scintillation count histograms for the full set of ISM files from the SA Agulhas II. As discussed in section 3.5, a Python script was used to count the number of scintillation events which exceeded the threshold value of 0.2 for both S_4 and σ_ϕ. The data problems were identified and fixed, and the corrected daily histograms were generated. The corrected S_{4c} values were used for amplitude scintillation, as shown in Figure 3.7.

The daily histograms showed large variations in the results, with no initial explanation. Some days were quiet, other days showed high counts throughout the day, while the rest had large spikes in the scintillation counts at intervals throughout the day. In order to establish a baseline, a daily histogram was generated using data from the closest fixed GISTM station which is located in Hermanus (HER) at the SANSA Space Science campus. The direct geographic separation between the SA Agulhas II GISTM and Hermanus GISTM is approximately 93.6 km.

A date was selected (10 October 2014) for which the SA Agulhas II was known to be stationary at the dock in Cape Town harbour in order to match the environmental conditions as closely as possible. The SA Agulhas II (AGLS2) data and the Hermanus (HER) data were overlaid as seen in Figure 4.1. The values for both both S_4 and σ_ϕ are significantly higher throughout the day for the SA Agulhas II (blue). The Hermanus data (red) had no σ_ϕ values exceeding the threshold of 0.2 rad, and very few instances where the S_4 values exceeded the threshold.

The source of the excessive readings from the SA Agulhas II was speculated to be caused by an environmental factor unique to the ship. Specifically, the movement of the SA Agulhas II was considered; even when docked the entire ship does have a small range of motion.

4.2.1 Daily histogram pattern analysis: SA Agulhas II

A series of daily histograms were generated for a period (1-17 February 2015) where the motion of the SA Agulhas II covered the entire range of possibilities: docked in the harbour, sailing on the open ocean, holding position in the middle of the ocean, and parked against the ice sheet of Antarctica. The daily histograms are shown in Figures 4.2-4.4. Additionally, the author was present aboard the vessel during this period and experienced these movements first-hand.

The SA Agulhas II was docked at the Akta Bukta ice shelf in Antarctica from 29 January 2015 until 1 February 2016 for initial cargo and crew loading operations. The ship appears deceptively stationary, however, maintaining a safe position against the ice within the artificially gouged dock requires regular and gentle but brief 'pushes' using the engines.

On 2 February 2015 the vessel moved away from the ice shelf to perform an assortment of manoeuvres up and down the coastline for oceanographic research purposes. This consists of long periods of quiet drifting for whale research, interspersed by bouts of sailing to the next whale target area. The ship may also engage the engines briefly for iceberg avoidance.

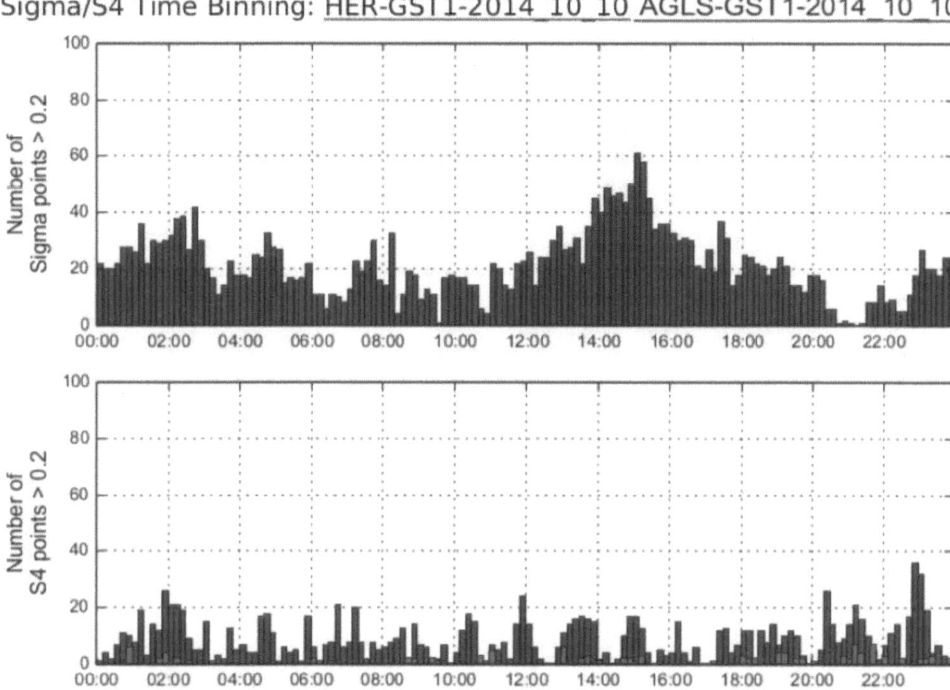

Figure 4.1: The combined daily histogram for Hermanus (red) and the SA Agulhas II (blue) recorded on 10 October 2014. Hermanus recorded no σ_ϕ threshold events; the few scattered S_4 threshold events did not exceed a count of 10 occurrences.

The SA Agulhas II returned to Akta Bukta for final loading of crew on 06 February 2015. It then set sail back to Cape Town, negotiating the ice until open water was reached and cruising speed could be achieved. On 10 February a series of oceanographic research sensors were hunted down and retrieved, and some additional experiments were collected.

On 11 February 2015 the SA Agulhas II stopped briefly at Bouvet Island to retrieve a team of scientists. The ship then continued on to Cape Town with no further stops. On 16 February 2015 the ship slowed to avoid arriving ahead of the scheduled docking time. It finally docked in Cape Town on the morning of 17 February 2015.

The overall pattern of σ_ϕ counts exceeding the threshold in the daily histograms bore a striking resemblance to the movement patterns of the SA Agulhas II during the same period. When the ship was stationary or drifting, the number of incidents were non-existent to low. When the ship performed slow to moderate movements, the incident count increased accordingly.

Strong acceleration and sustained high velocities reflected as overwhelming peaks and continuous high incident counts. The S_4 incident counts remained unaffected; no mimicry of the ship's motion, cyclic, or diurnal patterns were discerned visually.

The daily scintillation count histograms are derived from the ISM data files; the ship movements were documented anecdotally by the author on board the SA Agulhas II. The velocity of the SA Agulhas II can be plotted for the same period using the PSN data files in order to confirm the hypothesis that the motion of the ship introduces scintillation 'noise' in the σ_ϕ values.

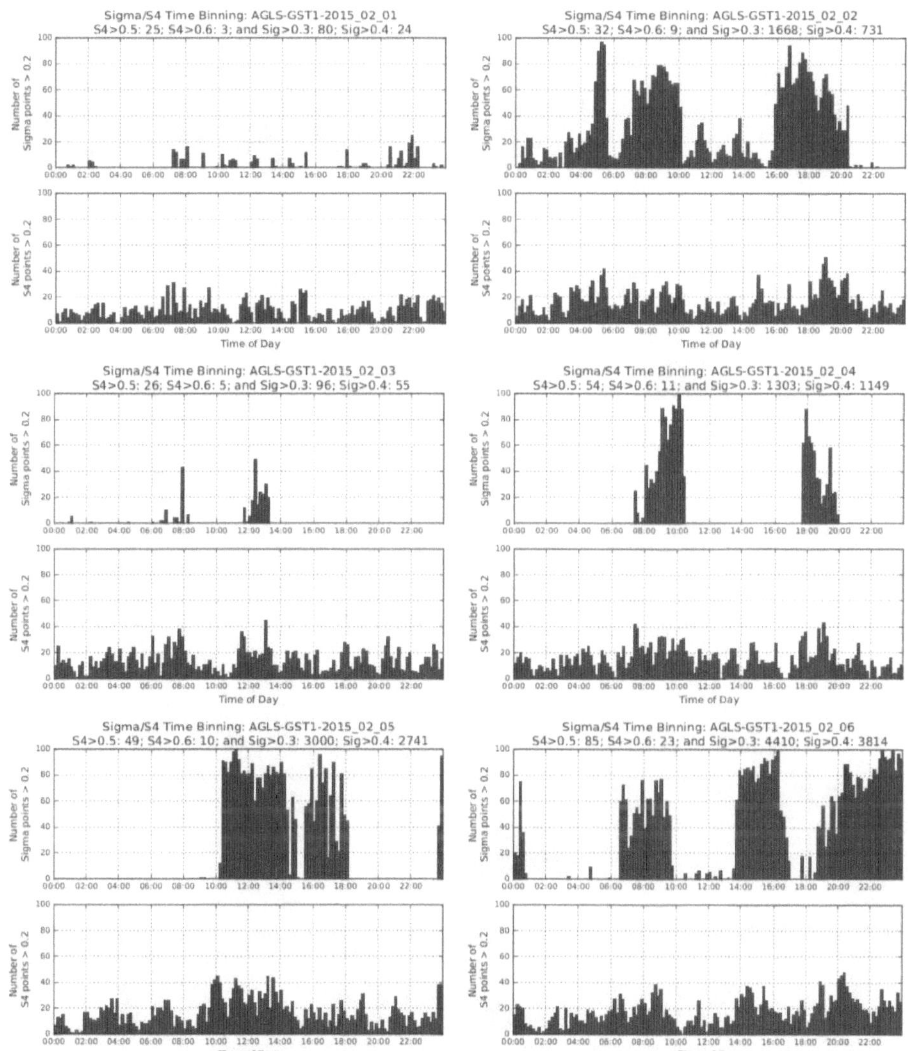

Figure 4.2: Daily histograms from the SA Agulhas II showing the number of S_4 and σ_ϕ values greater than 0.2 from 1-6 February 2015. The peaks and absences observed in the σ_ϕ counts show a remarkable visual correlation to the movement sequences undertaken by the SA Agulhas II during the same period.

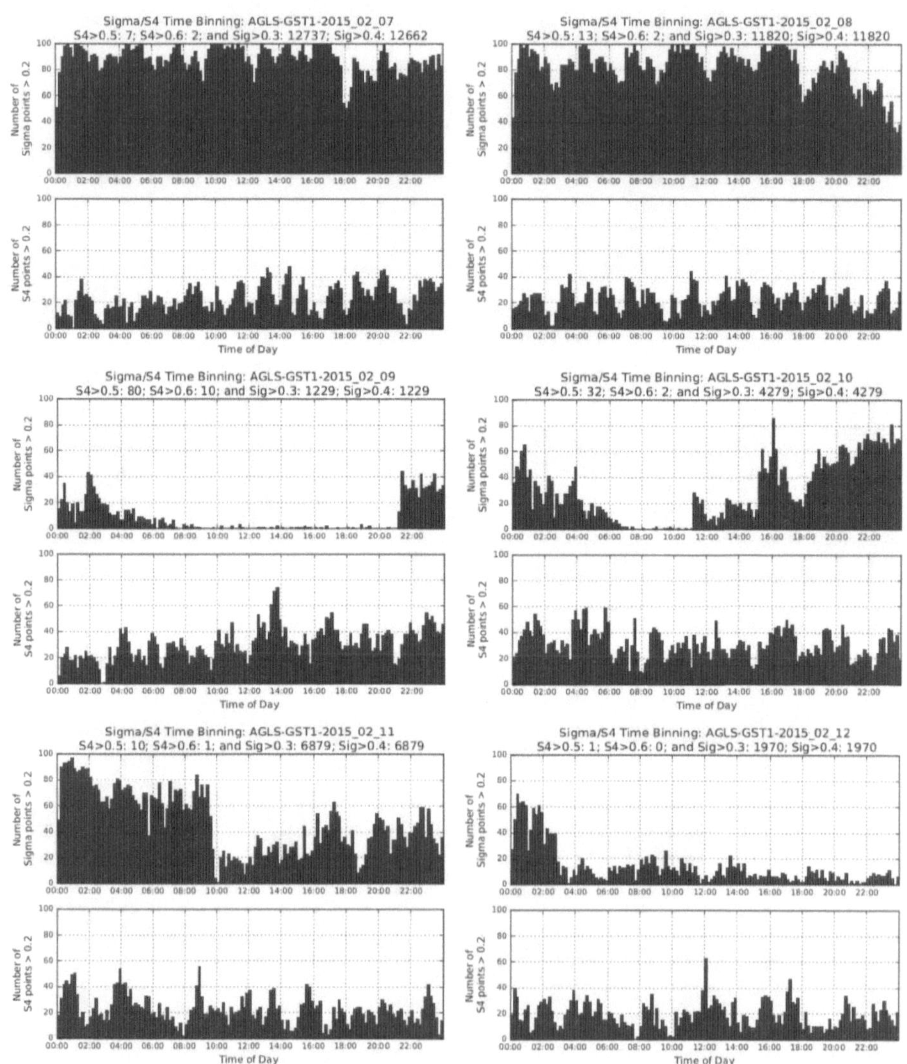

Figure 4.3: A continuation of daily histograms from the SA Agulhas II showing the number of S_4 and σ_ϕ values greater than 0.2 from 7-12 February 2015.

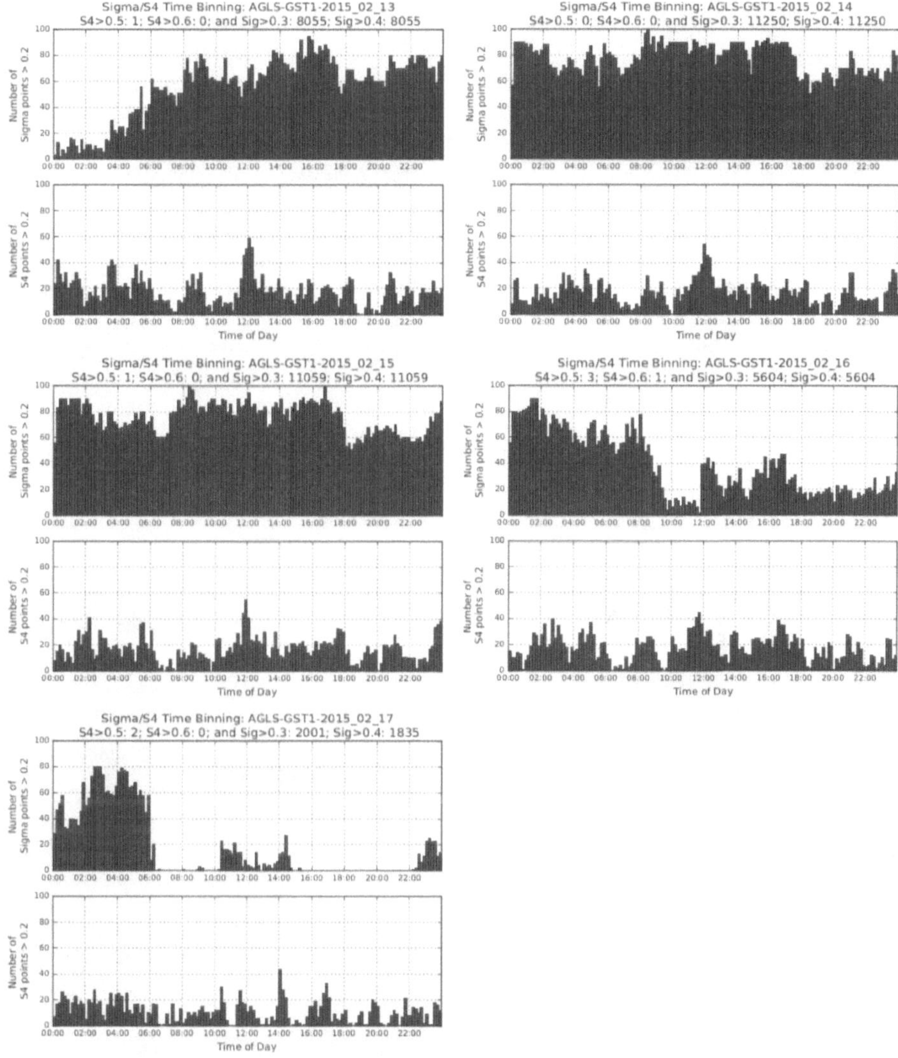

Figure 4.4: The final set of plots in the sequence of daily histograms from the SA Agulhas II showing the number of S_4 and σ_ϕ values greater than 0.2 as recorded from 13-17 February 2015.

4.3   Geographic and time constraints

Motion-induced noise may mask the presence of scintillation, so a stationary scintillation data set was obtained for comparison; preferably sourced from within the SAMA. The only option was Gough Island. The scintillation count histogram comparison between Hermanus and the SA Agulhas II in Cape Town Harbour had a separation distance of just under 100 km; for consistency the same distance was used as the maximum radius of the area of investigation between the SA Agulhas II and Gough Island.

The PSN files from the SA Agulhas II were then used to constrain the data to only locations within 100 km of Gough Island. Figure 4.5 shows the trajectory of the SA Agulhas II within this boundary during its 2015 voyage. The Gough Island ISM and PSN data files which matched the SA Agulhas II's trips to Gough Island were obtained from SANSA. The only overlapping data set available for both GISTMs were for the period 15-28 September 2015. A close-up of the trajectory for the SA Agulhas II within those dates overlaid on satellite imagery is shown in Figure 4.6.

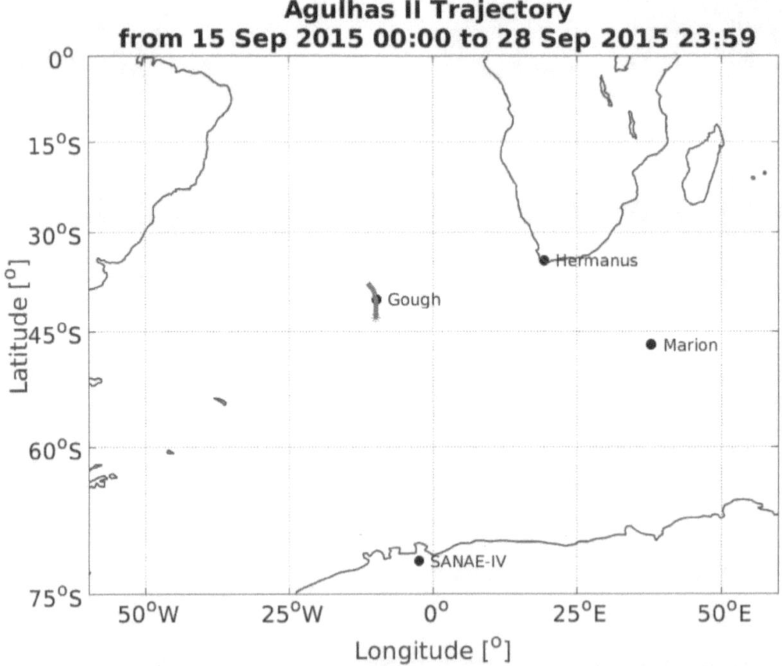

Figure 4.5: A map showing the SA Agulhas II sailing within 100km of Gough Island indicating the constrained data period to be 15-28 September 2015.

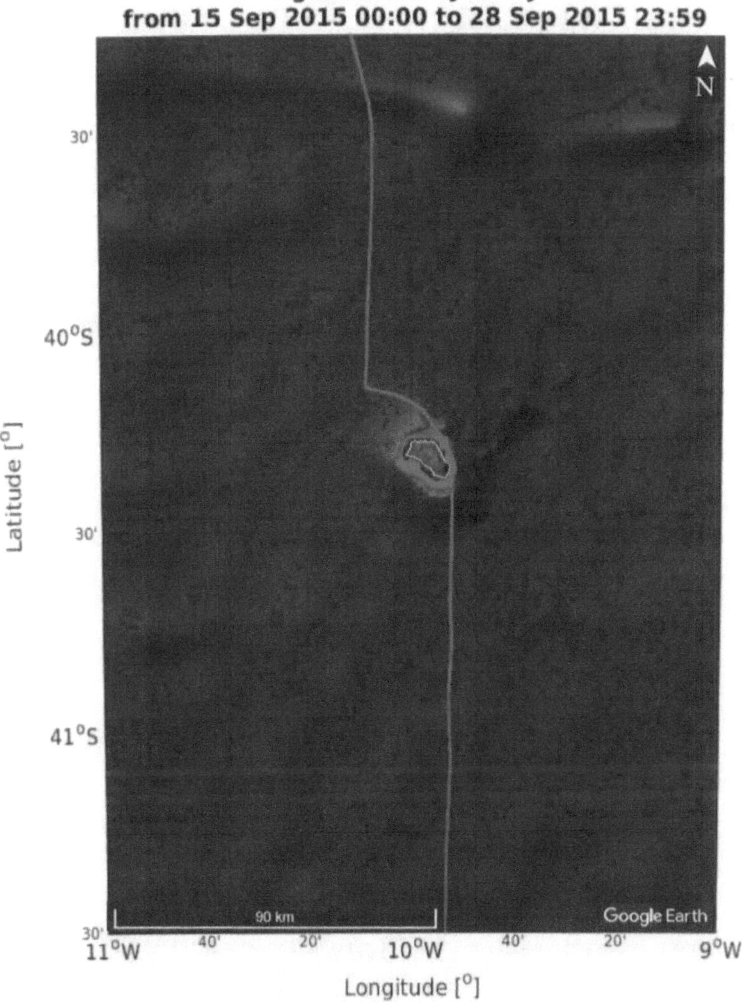

Figure 4.6: The northbound sailing trajectory of the SA Agulhas II within a 100km distance of Gough Island on 15-28 September 2015 overlaid with satellite imagery from Google Earth. The ship approached from the south and went around the island two or three times while intermittent cargo operations were underway.

4.4 Histogram comparison: Gough Island and SA Agulhas II

The daily scintillation count Python script was run using the Gough Island data for the overlapping period of 15-28 September 2015. This was done with 3 purposes:

- To test that the Gough Island GISTM had been functional and recording properly
- To ensure the Gough Island data did not contain errors like the SA Agulhas II experienced
- To establish a new baseline for the expected results in that area for the dates in question.

A side-by-side comparison of the Gough Island and SA Agulhas II daily histograms for 15 September 2015 is shown in Figure 4.7.

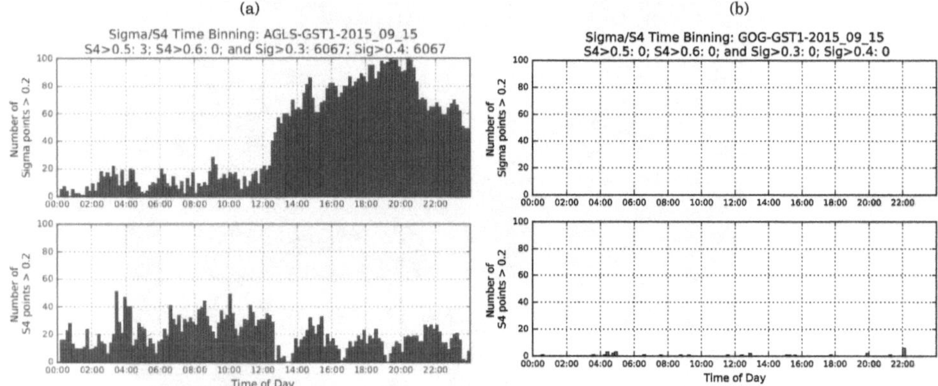

Figure 4.7: (a): A scintillation count histogram for the SA Agulhas II from 15 September 2015 is shown on the left. The scintillation counts are extremely high in the second half of the day; (b): A scintillation count histogram for Gough Island for the same day is shown on the right. Barely any scintillation counts are visible.

The SA Agulhas II histogram once again shows many instances of the threshold being crossed. The Gough Island histogram displays no recorded σ_ϕ values greater than 0.2 rad, and a minuscule number of S_4 events greater than 0.2. The Gough Island GISTM is the same hardware and software as the SA Agulhas II GISTM, however it is a fixed monitoring station. The data from this station can serve as a reliable indicator of the expected presence or absence of scintillation events in the SA Agulhas II GISTM data.

The excessive number of events recorded on the moving GISTM reinforces the hypothesis that the motion of the SA Agulhas II is a source of scintillation 'noise'.

4.5 MATLAB Analysis: ISM and PSN output graphs

A detailed overview of the MATLAB code developed for this research is available in Appendix A.2. The MATLAB code is a programmatic implementation of the various methods and equations outlined in Chapter 2, making use of the ISM and PSN data files described in Section 3.4.2 and Section 3.4.3 as input.

An example of each of the graphs generated using MATLAB is presented in the following sections. For convenience, both the SA Agulhas II graphs and the Gough Island graphs are shown together. All times of day referred to in the graphs are in UTC and written in 24-hour format. Each graph type has a unique Plot ID which was used in the MATLAB code. The Plot IDs are shown in the graph headings and captions.

4.5.1 Plot ID 1: Carrier-to-Noise Density ratio (C/N_o)

The Carrier-to-Noise Density ratio graphs (C/N_o) per PRN recorded from the SA Agulhas II and Gough Island are shown in Figure 4.8 (See Section 2.5.3 for the definition and equations). All the MATLAB graphs are generated separately, however these have been specifically combined to emphasise the differences recorded between Gough Island and the SA Agulhas II on 18 September 2015 (PRN27) and 20 September 2015 (PRN32).

The Gough Island C/N_o curves (blue) are good representations of the expected output. The values measured are in line with the typical C/N_o values for an L1 receiver. The C/N_o graph was generated individually for each PRN. The C/N_o graph is automatically zoomed to the period where the GPS satellite was visible in order to provide the highest level of detail.

On 18 September 2015 the SA Agulhas II PRN27 curves (red) show some short duration deep fades in the morning between roughly 07:30 and 08:10, and again between 08:30 and 08:45. The second visible period of PRN27 shows normal variations. The SA Agulhas II C/N_o curve for PRN32 on 20 September 2015 is another example of a short duration deep fade between approximately 09:30 and 09:45.

A strong dip such as the one seen in the SA Agulhas II C/N_o data may be an indicator of amplitude scintillation, and thus the C/N_o graph is one of the first proxies used to identify potential instances of scintillation events. This graph also illustrates the slight difference in observation capability between the Gough Island GISTM and the SA Agulhas II GISTM. The morning signal from PRN27 was lost by the Gough Island station nearly 30 minutes before the SA Agulhas II station disconnects. This is indicative of a difference in the line-of-sight between the two locations despite their close proximity.

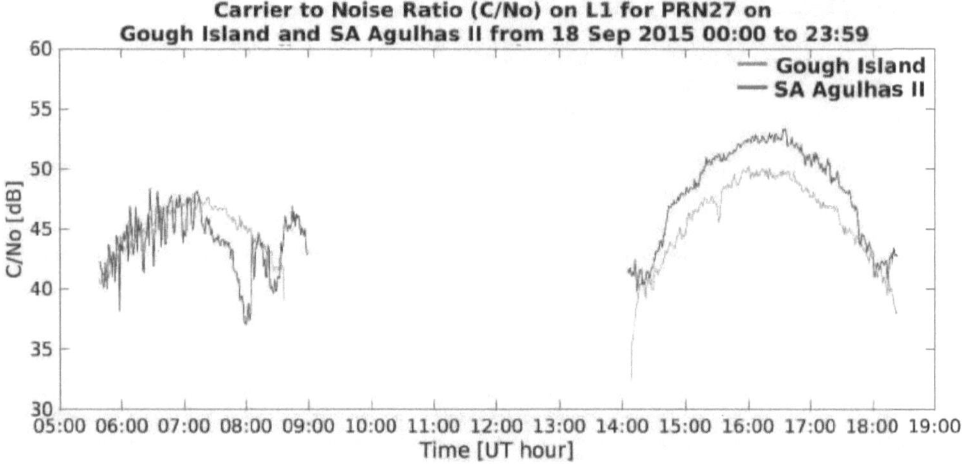

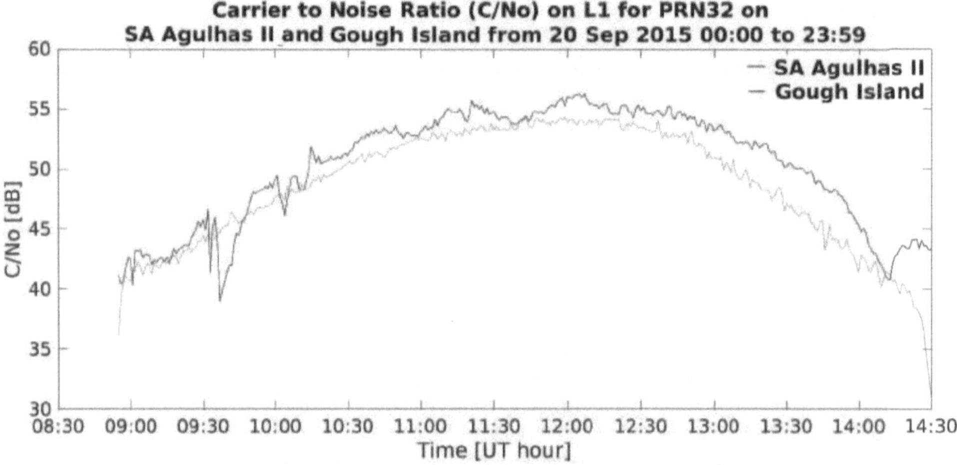

Figure 4.8: Plot ID 1: Examples of Carrier-to-Noise Density ratio (C/N_o) graphs. (Top): Combined C/N_o for PRN27 on 18 September 2015 showing both Gough Island (blue) data and SA Agulhas II (red) data. The satellite is visible twice during the day. The SA Agulhas II values show a significant drop between 07:00 and 08:00, and another at roughly 08:30 which is not visible in the Gough Island data. (Bottom): A combined C/N_o graph for PRN32 on 20 September 2015 displaying Gough Island (blue) data and SA Agulhas II (red) data. PRN32 is only visible once during the day. A sharp drop is visible between 09:30-09:45 from the SA Agulhas II while the Gough Island curve remains unaffected.

4.5.2 Plot ID 2: L1 Lock Time and Elevation (all PRN) graphs

The L1 Lock Time and Elevation graphs for all PRNs recorded from the SA Agulhas II and on Gough Island are shown in Figure 4.9. Lock time is discussed in Section 2.5.2 and the expected visibility of GPS satellites is covered in Section 2.5.5.

The observed pattern of satellite elevations as viewed from Gough Island for 15 September 2015 was validated against the expected satellite visibility graph drawn using the Trimble software for the same day (see Figure 2.11). The similarity of the SA Agulhas II and Gough Island elevation graphs indicate that the two GISTM receivers were locking onto the same satellites.

The L1 lock time graph shows continuous linear increases in the count of the time elapsed since satellite acquisition. These coincide with the corresponding satellite rising above the 10° horizon as seen in the accompanying elevation graph. The lock time and elevation graphs from Gough Island present an example of the simultaneous loss of lock and loss of visibility of all the GPS satellites between 15:50-17:20.

This particular interruption in GISTM data from Gough Island was planned; shortly after the ship's arrival at Gough Island on 15 September 2015, an engineer turned off the receiver unit to conduct mainte-nance activities. At 18:15 a second reboot (power cycling) of the receiver unit was performed, leading to a brief loss of lock which reset the L1 lock time counts again. Scintillation-induced loss of lock will usually only affect one satellite, not all of the connected satellites.

4.5.3 Plot ID 3: L1 Lock Time and Elevation (single PRN) graphs

The L1 Lock Time and Elevation graphs for a single satellite, PRN 7, are shown in Figure 4.10 for both the SA Agulhas II and Gough Island. When a single PRN is selected for investigation the axes of the graph are automatically adjusted to the period in which the satellite is visible. PRN 7 was visible only once on 15 September 2015 between 14:30-21:00.

The maintenance work performed on the Gough Island GISTM from 15:50-17:20 as well as the second reboot at 18:15 occurred during the PRN 7 transit. The data gap and the two resets of the L1 lock time count are clearly visible. Loss of lock with a single satellite because of scintillation would look very much like the second lock time reset presented here; the satellite signal would be re-acquired quickly, but a 240 s buffer period for the signal to fully converge is recommended before making use of the data for analysis.

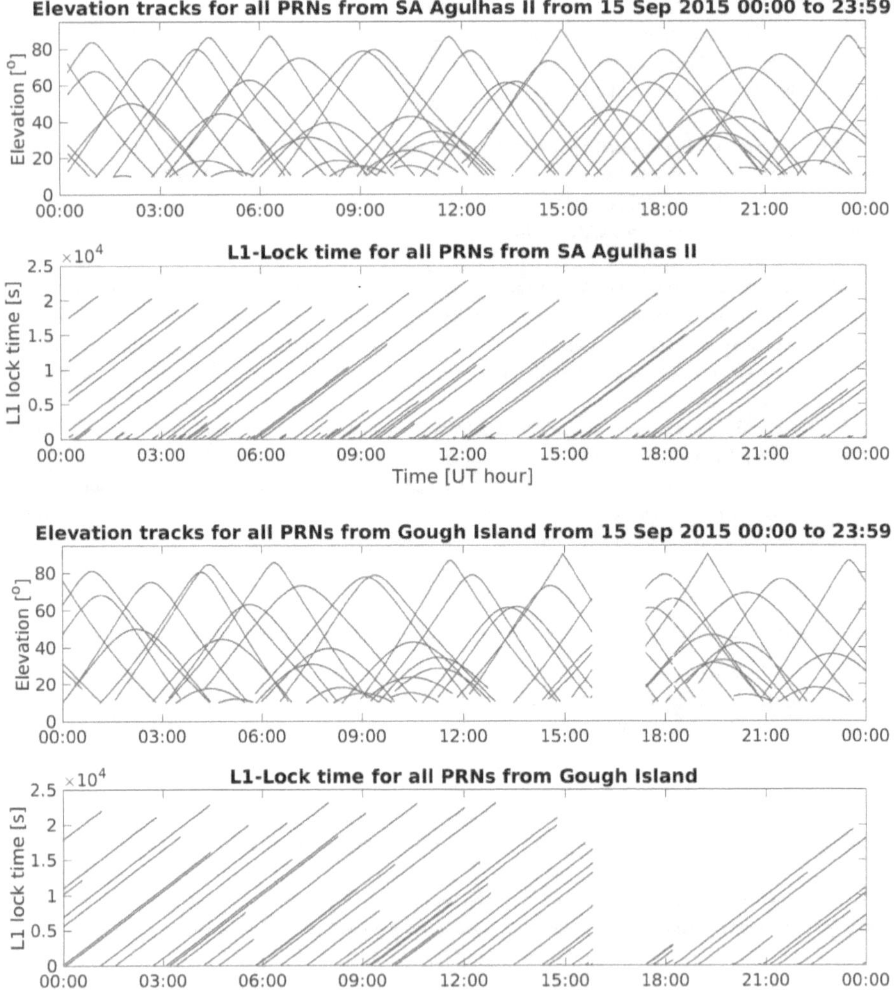

Figure 4.9: Plot ID 2: An example of the L1 Lock Time and Elevation graphs from 15 September 2015. (Top): The elevation tracks of all the GPS satellites as seen from the SA Agulhas II with the corresponding L1 lock time graph below. The SA Agulhas II lock time graph has several very short lock time lines which do not appear in the Gough Island graph. (Bottom): Elevation tracks from Gough Island for all GPS satellites with corresponding lock time graph below. The complete interruption in the data for both graphs is a result of planned power loss on the Gough Island GISTM receiver.

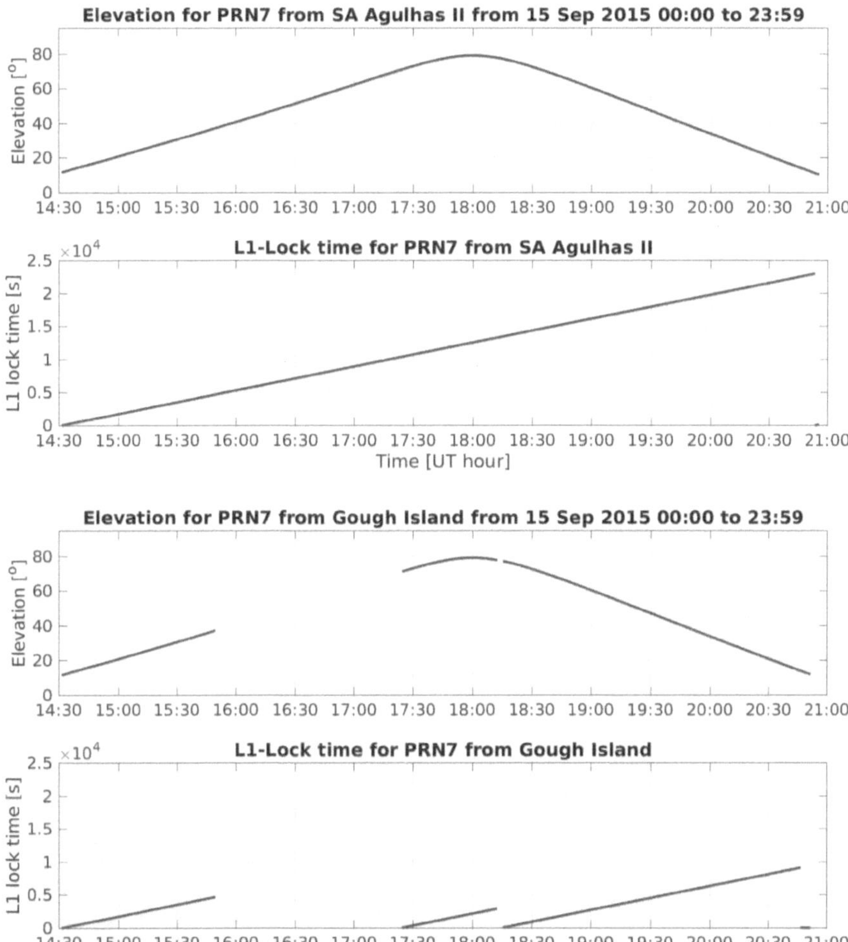

Figure 4.10: Plot ID 3: Examples of single-PRN L1 Lock Time and Elevation graphs from the SA Agulhas II and Gough Island, for PRN 7 on 15 September 2015. (Top): PRN 7 was visible between 14:30 and 21:00 without interruption from the SA Agulhas II, and passed nearly directly overhead (80°) at 18:00. The L1 lock time count is a single, continuous, linear increase and represents a perfect satellite pass. (Bottom): PRN 7 was similarly visible from Gough Island, however the planned power loss on the GISTM is clearly visible in the missing data. The resets of the L1 lock time count back to zero upon re-acquisition of the satellite are easily identified in this example graph.

4.5.4 Plot ID 10: Raw S_4 (all PRN) graphs

Figure 4.11 shows an example of the graphs generated from the raw S_4 (amplitude scintillation) observations from the SA Agulhas II and Gough Island on 15 September 2015. The measurement of S_4 is discussed in Section 2.3.4. The raw S_4 values range between 0 and 1, and include ambient noise effects and other errors (see Section 2.3.4).

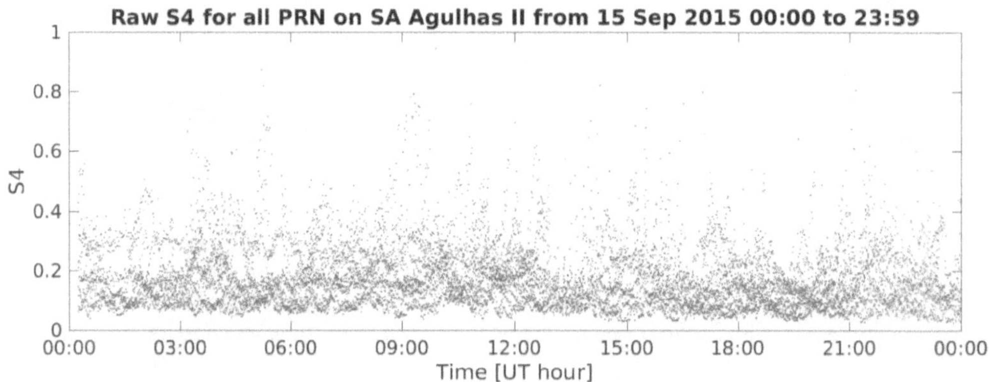

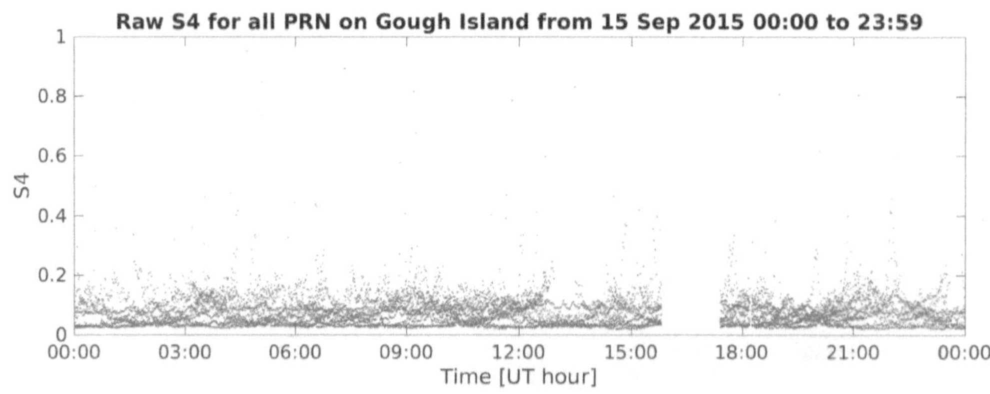

Figure 4.11: Plot ID 10: An example of the raw S_4 recorded from all PRN on 15 September 2015. (Top): In this instance, the raw S_4 measurements from the SA Agulhas II are larger and appear scattered compared to the Gough Island measurements. (Bottom): The raw S_4 recorded from Gough Island is lower than the SA Agulhas II observations, with the majority of the values falling below 0.2. The power loss on the Gough Island GISTM is again clearly visible by the gap in the data.

4.5.5 Plot ID 11: Elevation vs S_{4c} multi-pane (all PRN) graphs

The multi-pane graphs shown in Figure 4.12 are examples of the comparison between the elevation and the corrected S_{4c} calculated for each individual GPS satellite (see Section 2.3.4). These 32-pane graphs are for observations from the SA Agulhas II and on Gough Island on 15 September 2015. The S_{4c} values are expected to peak at low elevations and this trend is clearly visible at the edges of each satellite elevation track.

The S_{4c} axis lies on the right and ranges between 0 and 1. The left axis is the elevation above the horizon between 0° and 90° . The purpose of constructing a 32-pane graph is to easily compare all the PRNs to look for indicators of unusual behaviour on a given day. Spikes in the S_{4c} values while a satellite is at higher elevations may indicate the presence of a scintillation event.

4.5.6 Plot ID 13: Corrected S_{4c} (all PRN) graphs

After the raw S_4 values undergo correction as discussed in Section 2.3.4 the S_{4c} values are plotted as shown in Figure 4.13. The example shows S_{4c} for 15 September 2015 from the SA Agulhas II and on Gough Island for all PRN. With the removal and adjustments made to the amplitude scintillation data during processing, the number of data points in the graph is expected to reduce. This gives the S_{4c} graph better visual clarity than the raw S_4 as the clutter is removed.

The S_{4c} values range between 0 and 1. The data gaps in the Gough Island GISTM data from the power loss and the reboot during maintenance is clearly visible.

4.5.7 Plot ID 20: Raw σ_ϕ (all PRN) graphs

The example graphs for the raw σ_ϕ (phase scintillation) observations (see Section 2.3.5) from the SA Agulhas II and on Gough Island for 15 September 2015 are shown in Figure 4.14. The raw σ_ϕ values are measured in radians and the range of the y-axis is between 0 and 30. The high upper limit was selected in order to display all the σ_ϕ values on the graph. As discussed in Section 4.1.2, σ_ϕ values of 0.26 are considered high scintillation conditions.

The unusual behaviour of the raw σ_ϕ data recorded from the SA Agulhas II on this particular day is discussed in greater detail in Chapter 5.

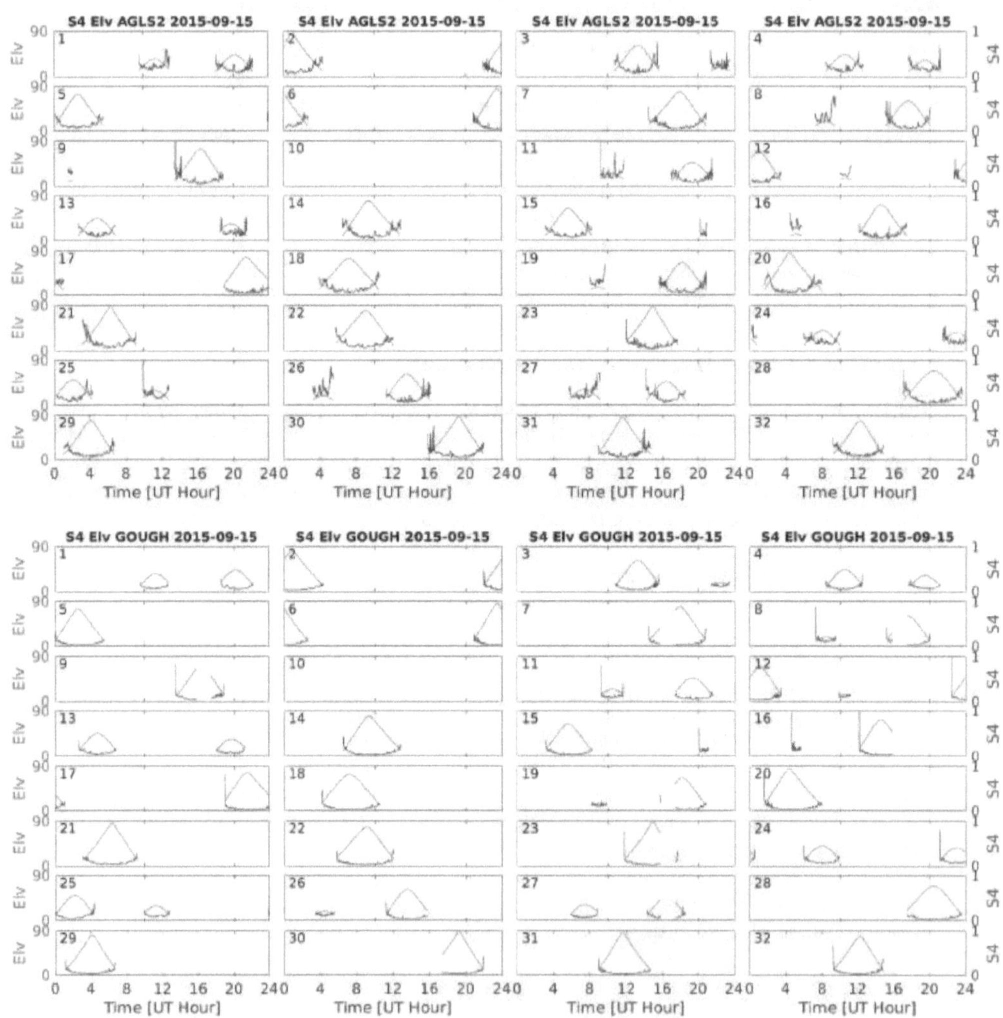

Figure 4.12: Plot ID 11: This graph is a combination of the S_{4c} and satellite elevation observations per PRN in a multi-pane format. The example shown is from 15 September 2015. (Top): The S_{4c} observations from the SA Agulhas II are larger and more volatile than the Gough Island readings. (Bottom): The S_{4c} curves from Gough Island are quieter, but still show the expected spikes at the edges of the elevation tracks.

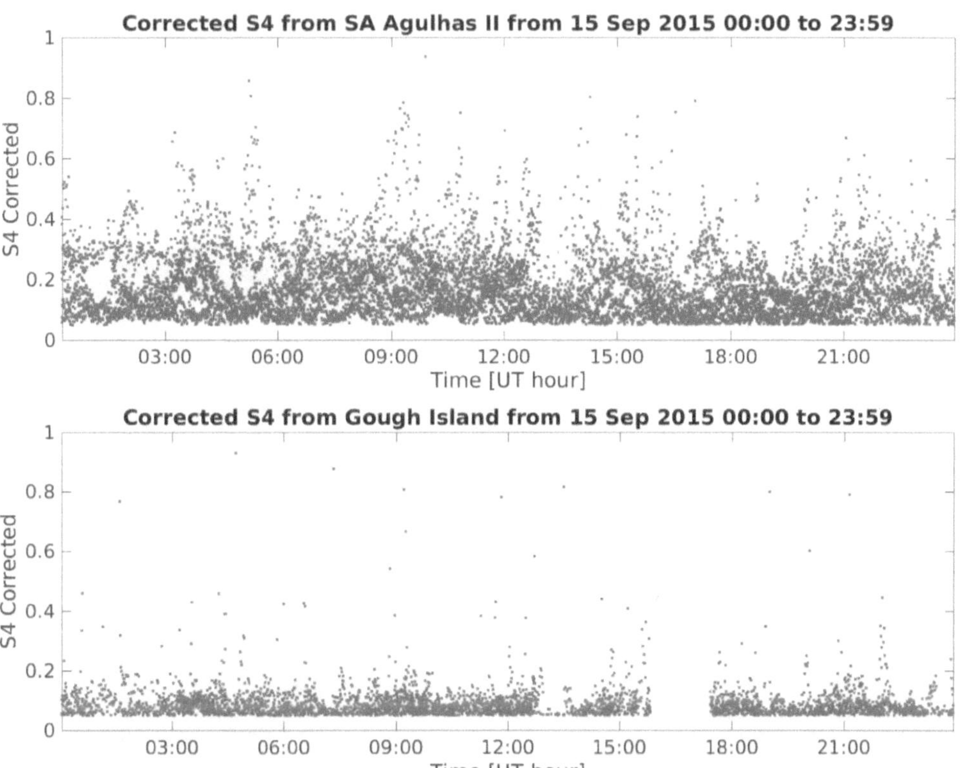

Figure 4.13: Plot ID 13: This example shows a graph of the corrected S_{4c} across all
PRN on 15 September 2015. (Top): The S_{4c} measurements from the SA Agulhas II
are still larger than, and still scattered compared to the Gough Island measurements.
Some noise has been removed and the graph has more clarity than the raw S_4 graph.
(Bottom): The corrected S_{4c} for Gough Island is lower than the S_{4c} observations for
the SA Agulhas II. The removal of noise is visible as most of the data points below
the threshold value of 0.05 have been eliminated. The power losses of the Gough
Island GISTM are clearly visible by the gap in the data.

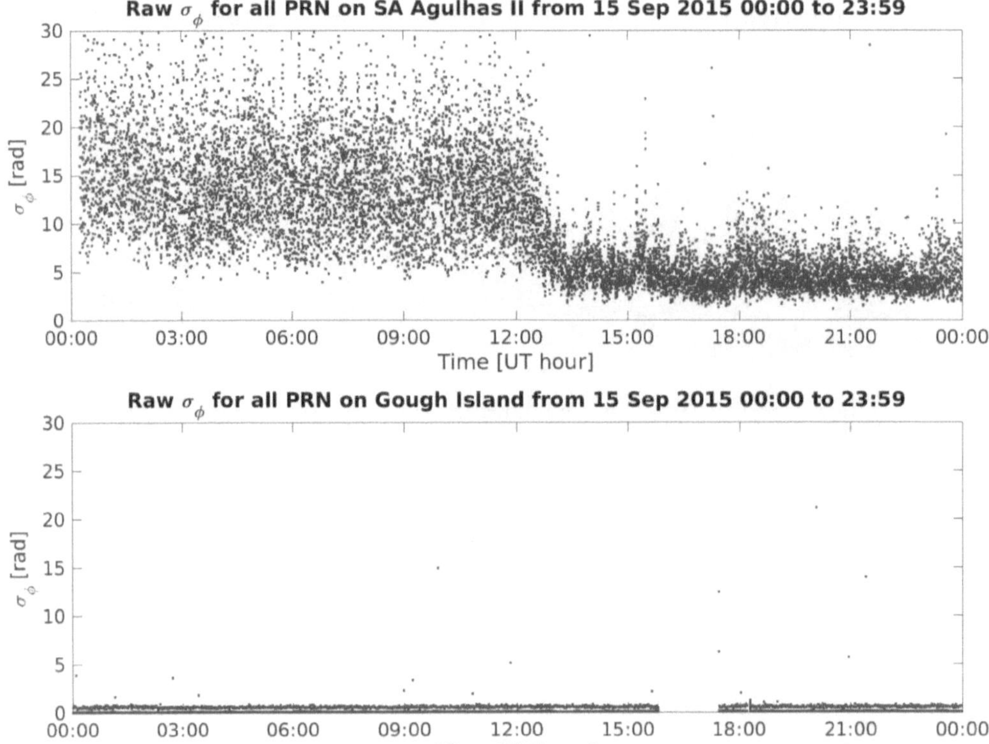

Figure 4.14: Plot ID 20: An example of the raw σ_ϕ recorded across all PRN for 15 September 2015. (Top): The raw σ_ϕ measurements from the SA Agulhas II show a wide distribution with extraordinarily high values up to 30 rad, especially in the hours leading up to 13:00. After 13:00 the raw σ_ϕ values have a narrower distribution, with the majority of the values below 10 rad. The reason for this change in distribution is unknown. (Bottom): By comparison, most of the raw σ_ϕ values from Gough Island are below 1 rad; only 16 sporadic data points are above 1 rad, and there is no visible change in the data at 13:00 as with the ship's data. The power loss data gap for the Gough Island GISTM is visible yet again.

4.5.8   Plot ID 22: Elevation vs. σ_ϕ multi-pane (all PRN) graphs

The multi-pane graphs shown in Figure 4.15 are the elevation vs. σ_ϕ equivalent of 4.12. The 32-pane graphs are an easy way to compare the σ_ϕ and elevation tracks for all the individual GPS satellites with each other. This example shows data recorded on 15 September 2015 from the SA Agulhas II and Gough Island. This example shows the change in the range of the σ_ϕ values before and after 13:00 across all satellites. An example of a coinciding σ_ϕ spike pattern is visible at 16:00 across four different satellites with elevations well above the horizon (PRNs 9, 16, 23, and 27).

The σ_ϕ values have been corrected using a combination of outlier and anomalous data removal, filtering out of low elevation values, and application of the selected scintillation thresholds.

4.5.9   Plot ID 23: Corrected σ_ϕ (all PRN) graphs

The corrected σ_ϕ observations for 15 September 2015 from the SA Agulhas II and Gough Island are shown in Figure 4.16. This graph follows on from the raw σ_ϕ graph (Figure 4.14). The corrections made to the σ_ϕ values are discussed in Section 4.5.8. The effect of the filtering is more clearly seen in the Gough Island σ_ϕ data than the SA Agulhas II data compared to the raw data.

The σ_ϕ values are measured in radians, and the y-axis ranges from 0 to 30. As seen with the raw σ_ϕ graph (Figure 4.14), the SA Agulhas II data exhibits highly unusual behaviour after approximately 13:00. This behaviour is discussed in Section 4.5.15.

4.5.10   Plot ID 24: Corrected σ_ϕ (single PRN) graphs

The corrected σ_ϕ values for a single PRN are shown in the example graph seen in Figure 4.17. The data is from 15 September 2015 as recorded on the SA Agulhas II and on Gough Island. When an individual PRN is selected for investigation the axes are automatically adjusted to only the period when the satellite was visible; in this example PRN 7 was visible between 14:30-21:00.

The data gaps resulting from the Gough Island GISTM maintenance work are visible, however the σ_ϕ values are so small that they are barely visible at this scale. The SA Agulhas II graph provides a clearer view of how distributed the recorded σ_ϕ values are, even during the unusual quieter phase experienced by the ship after 13:00.

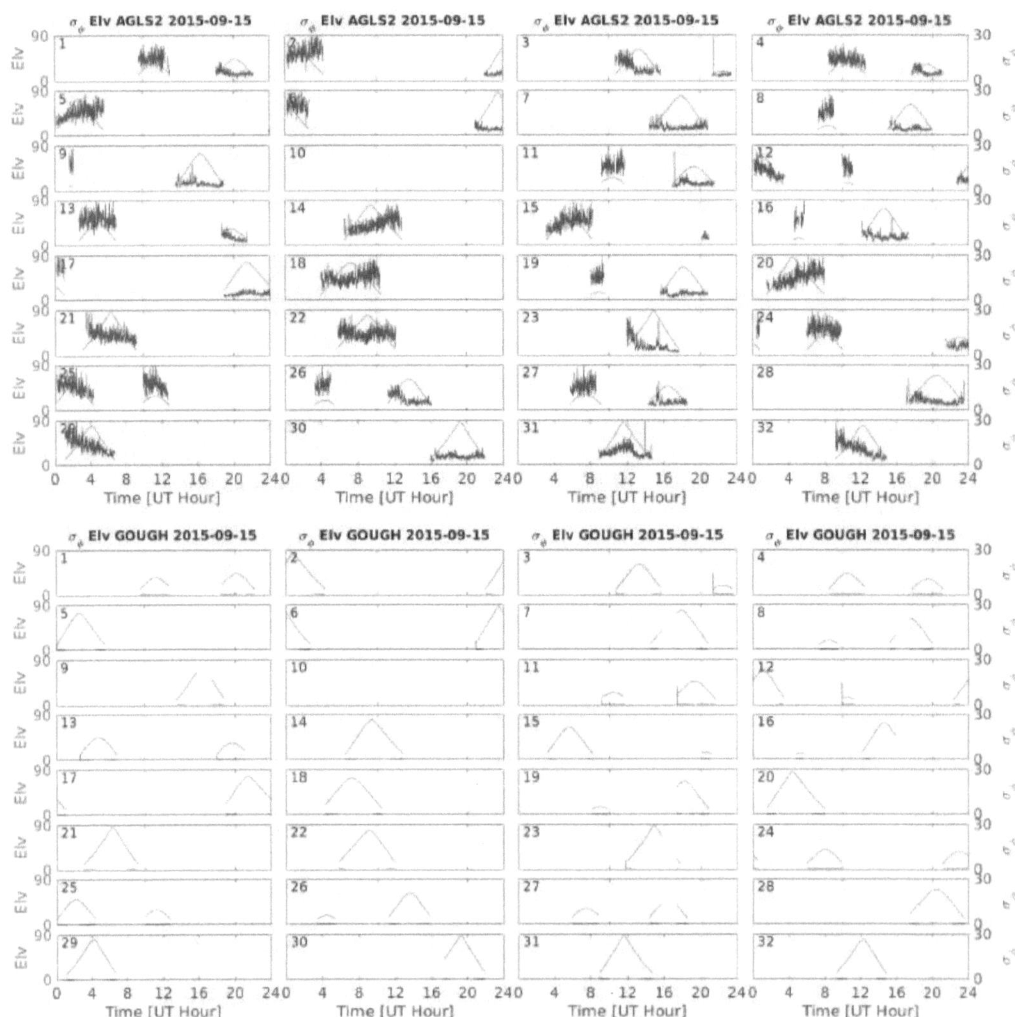

Figure 4.15: Plot ID 22: This graph combines the corrected σ_ϕ and elevation for each PRN in a 32-pane format, recorded on 15 September 2015 from the SA Agulhas II and Gough Island. (Top): The SA Agulhas II data is extremely noisy compared to the Gough Island graph, especially before 13:00. After 13:00 the values are inexplicably lower. Peculiar spikes at 16:00 are observed simultaneously in the σ_ϕ values of PRNs 9, 16, 23, and 27. All four satellites are at reasonably high elevations, with PRN 27 being the lowest at 40°. PRN 3 appears unaffected at a 20° elevation. (Bottom): The σ_ϕ curves for Gough Island are almost invisible except for a few narrow spikes which coincide with the rising of PRNs 3, 11, 12, and 23.

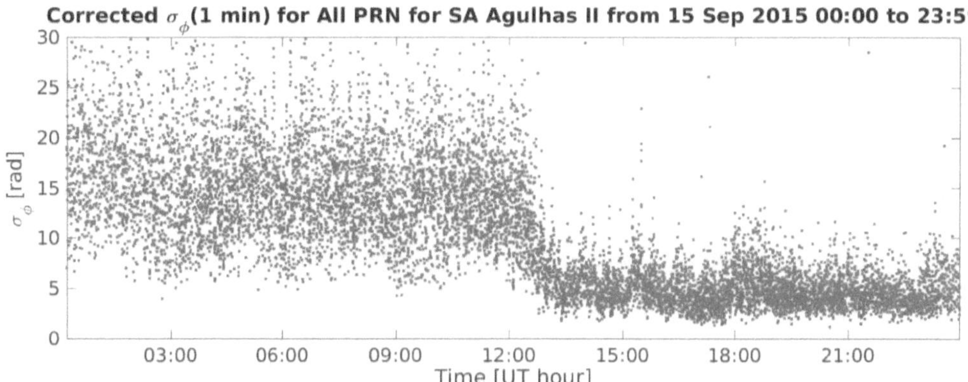

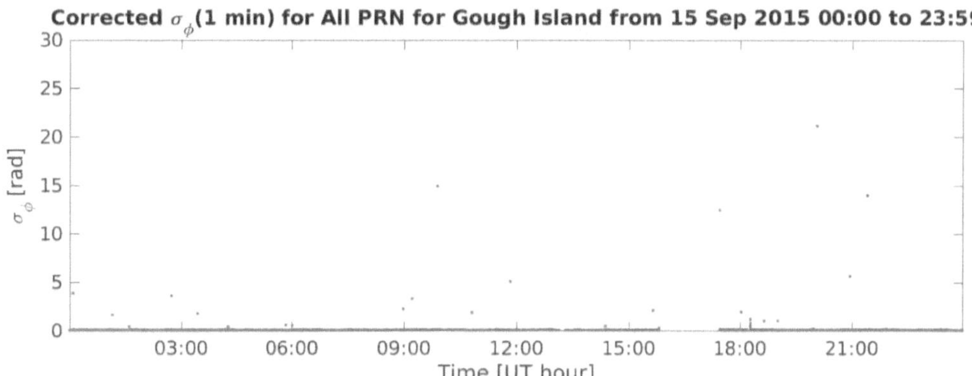

Figure 4.16: Plot ID 23: An example of the corrected σ_ϕ values for all PRN measured from the SA Agulhas II and on Gough Island on 15 September 2015 is shown. (Top): The corrected σ_ϕ values for the SA Agulhas II still maintain the wide distribution seen in the raw data, and only a few data points have been removed. The unusual change in pattern from 13:00 is identical to the behaviour of the raw σ_ϕ graph, dropping from values of up to 30 rad down to values below 15 rad. (Bottom): The effect of the filtering is more visible in the corrected σ_ϕ from Gough Island, and the GISTM maintenance data gap remains present.

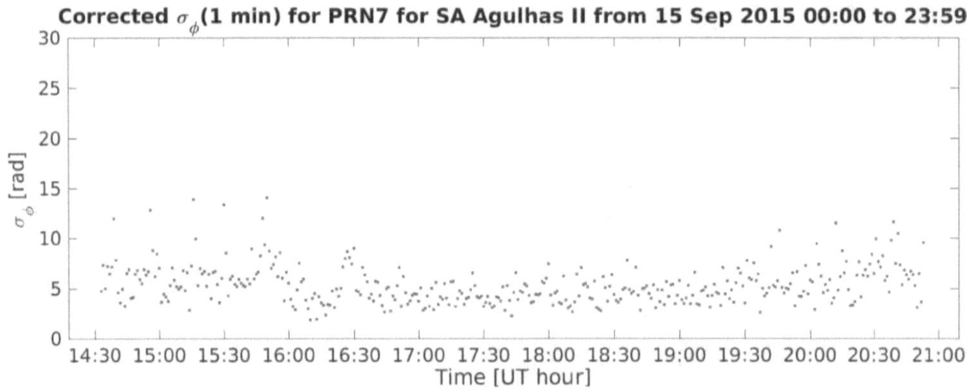

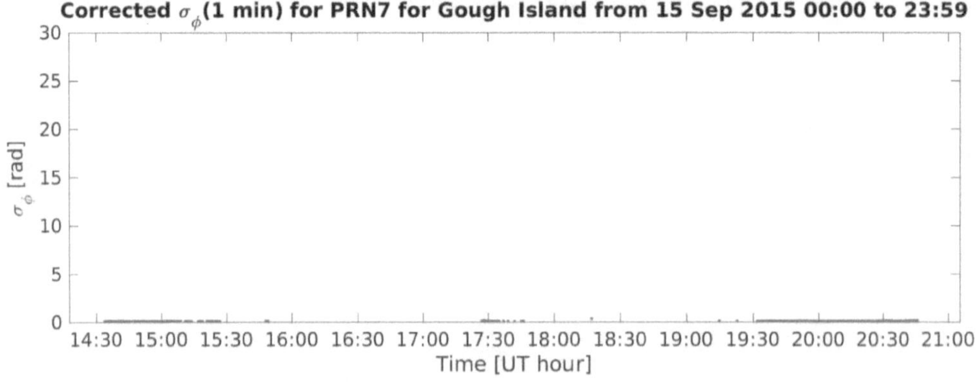

Figure 4.17: Plot ID 24: An example of the corrected σ_ϕ values for only PRN 7 from 15 September 2015 is shown here. The satellite was only visible between 14:30 and 21:00. (Top): The adjusted axes provide a clearer view of the σ_ϕ during the period of unusual quiet behaviour seen from the SA Agulhas II; no values are above 15 rad and the bulk range between 2-10 rad. (Bottom): PRN 7 was in transit during the Gough Island GISTM maintenance, but the power-down gap is essentially indistinguishable from periods where there were simply no σ_ϕ values above the threshold to display.

4.5.11 Plot ID 25: Corrected S_{4c} (single PRN) graphs

The corrected S_{4c} values shown in example Figure 4.18 highlight a single satellite, PRN 7. The axes are automatically scaled to display only the period in which the satellite was visible. This data was recorded on 15 September 2015 from the SA Agulhas II and on Gough Island. At low elevations, the S_{4c} values are expected to increase as the power intensity of the received signal is affected by the greater distance between the orbital transmitter and the terrestrial receiver.

The maintenance work on the Gough Island GISTM took place during this transit, and no data was recorded during that period. However, even after the system was operational, very few S_{4c} values exceeding the threshold were recorded. The maintenance gap is indistinguishable from a general lack of scintillation data, and thus it is important to review the individual graphs in the context of the bigger picture. Confusion between external factors and actual ionospheric conditions may occur both where data is present as well as where data is lacking.

4.5.12 Plot ID 30: Slant TEC (all PRN) graphs

The graphs shown in Figure 4.19 are typical examples of the Slant Total Electron Content (STEC) calculated from data recorded from the SA Agulhas II and on Gough Island. All PRNs are shown for 15 September 2015. STEC is measured in TECU and the axes range between 40 and 180 TECU. A daily maximum is expected at 14:00 in accordance with the known TEC behaviour of the ionosphere (see Section 2.4 for details) and the example graph is in accordance with this prediction.

The STEC values used in these graphs are uncorrected; normally an offset is calculated using a curve fitting algorithm to remove the effect of multipath errors and system noise (Horvath and Crozier, 2007). For this research, the corrected values of the STEC are not important; rapid changes in value or 'ripples' in the pattern of the curves are used to identify potential scintillation events. Calculating and applying the offset to the STEC data in order to correct it properly was thus not necessary.

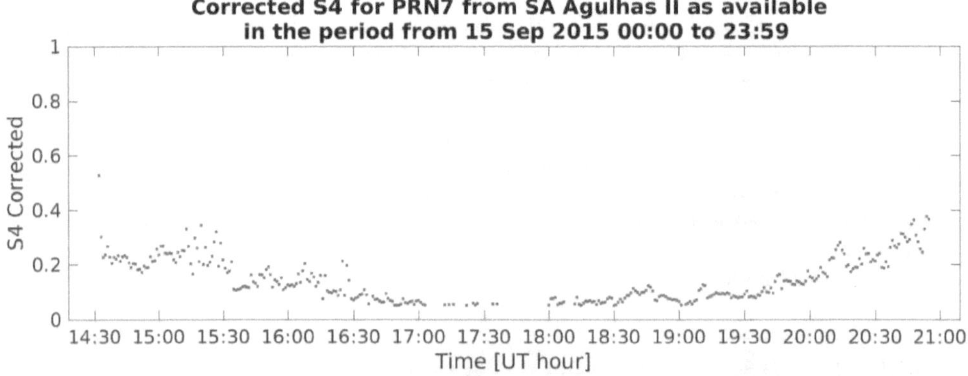

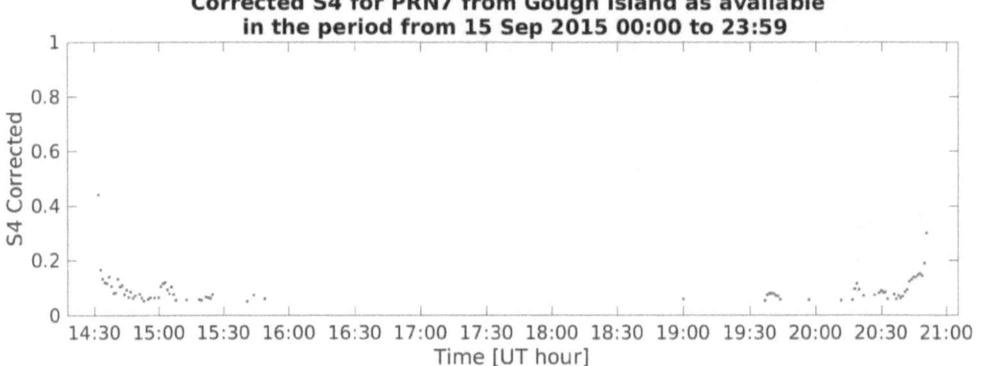

Figure 4.18: Plot ID 25: This is an example of a corrected S_{4c} graph for PRN 7 as recorded from the SA Agulhas II and on Gough Island on 15 September 2015 during the visible transit of the individual satellite. (Top): The S_{4c} curve from the SA Agulhas II is a clear example of the expected pattern for S_{4c} data; the S_{4c} is expected to increase at the rising and setting elevations of the satellite transit. The SA Agulhas II data still shows very large values for S_{4c} compared to the data from Gough Island. (Bottom): The S_{4c} values during the transit of PRN 7 as recorded on Gough Island also demonstrate the increase in S_{4c} expected at low elevations. The maintenance work does produce a gap in the data, however very few S_{4c} values above the threshold are seen even after the GISTM was working again.

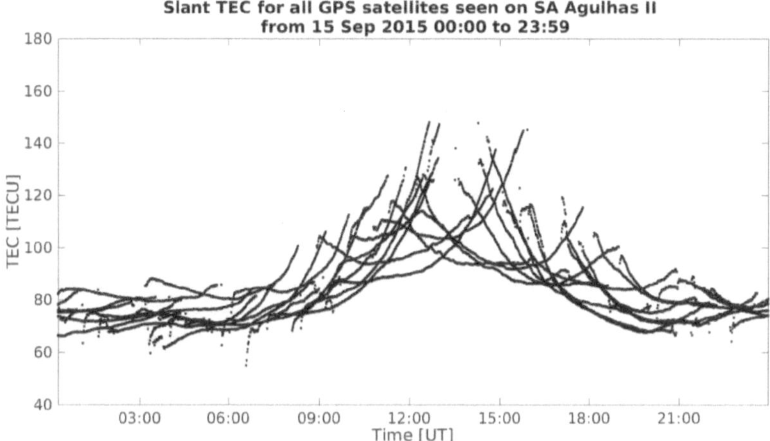

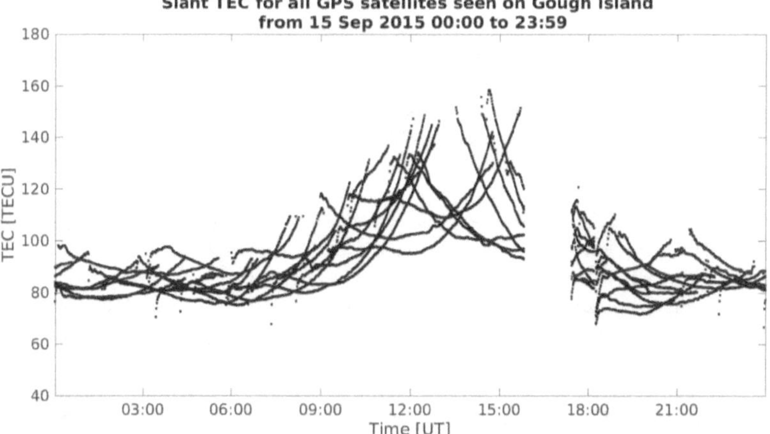

Figure 4.19: Plot ID 30: An example of a typical STEC graph is shown. The pattern of the combination of curves from all PRN for 15 September 2015 conforms to the expected pattern for global STEC, with a diurnal maximum at 14:00. (Top): The STEC values from the SA Agulhas II range between roughly 65 TECU at minimum and 150 TECU at the daily peak. (Bottom): The Gough Island STEC observations are slightly higher than those from the ship; they range between roughly 75 TECU at minimum and 160 TECU at maximum. The difference between the two locations is roughly 10 TECU. The patterns of the two graphs are the most important feature; the curves are fairly well matched with only minor variations between the SA Agulhas II data and the Gough Island data. As STEC is based on satellite-receiver geometry, these negligible differences are attributed to the slight difference in physical location. The GISTM maintenance gap is also clearly visible.

4.5.13 Plot ID 31: Vertical TEC (all PRN) graphs

Figure 4.20 shows examples of the Vertical Total Electron Content (VTEC) graphs generated in this research using data from the SA Agulhas II and on Gough Island recorded on 15 September 2015 for all PRN. VTEC is also measured in TECU (see Section 2.4) and is derived by multiplying the STEC by a mapping function which assumes 350 km as the ionospheric pierce point (IPP) altitude of the ray path (Horvath and Crozier, 2007) to scale the STEC to the equivalent VTEC. This was done in MATLAB using a function called slm2.m which takes the zenith angle and IPP height and performs the geometric calculation.

The red line in the VTEC graph is the mean calculated using a low order polynomial fit for the full day of VTEC data to facilitate the identification of scintillation events. As with the STEC graph, the actual VTEC values are not important in this research; 'ripples' in the curve patterns and rapid fluctuations in the VTEC value are the focus. The smoothed nature of the VTEC curves make it easier to identify such events in the search for potential scintillation.

4.5.14 Plot ID 50: GPS Satellite Visibility (all PRN) graphs

The visibility of all the GPS satellites in the sky from the SA Agulhas II and from Gough Island on 15 September 2015 is shown in Figure 4.21. The purpose of these plots is to confirm that the same satellites are visible from both locations. The line-of-sight between the satellite and the receiver is dependent on geography; it is expected that Edinburgh Peak (910 m) and Expedition Peak (909 m) on Gough Island will cause additional low-elevation obstructions. The SA Agulhas II is not expected to present any obstructions. Only elevations above 10° are shown.

The satellite visibility graph is an all-sky plot; the x-axis is azimuth (degrees) and ranges from 0° to 360° (North). The South Pole is at 180° from the receiver location. As a receiver moves south the relative orbits of the GPS satellites shift towards the north, resulting in a gap in the visibility map around the 180° area. Only high elevation (y-axis) GPS satellites will be visible in a southerly direction. The MATLAB code allows for a specific PRN to be highlighted if desired. In this example, the red highlighted track is for PRN 7.

The satellite visibility map does not have a temporal component; interruptions and disjointed tracks are not indicators of loss of lock. Instead the graph shows all the orbital tracks of the satellites in the sky from a specific location over the entire 24-hours of the selected day. A mid-sky start or discontinuation of a satellite track is most likely because the local time at which that satellite was in that position was 00:00. This is the last graph generated using the ISM data file.

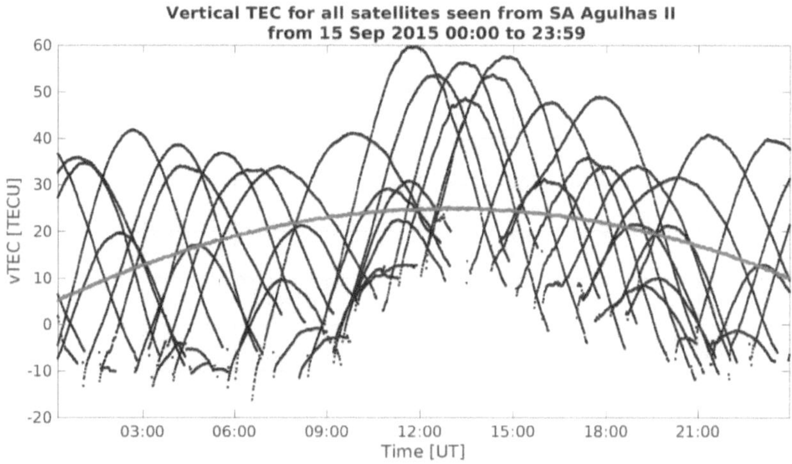

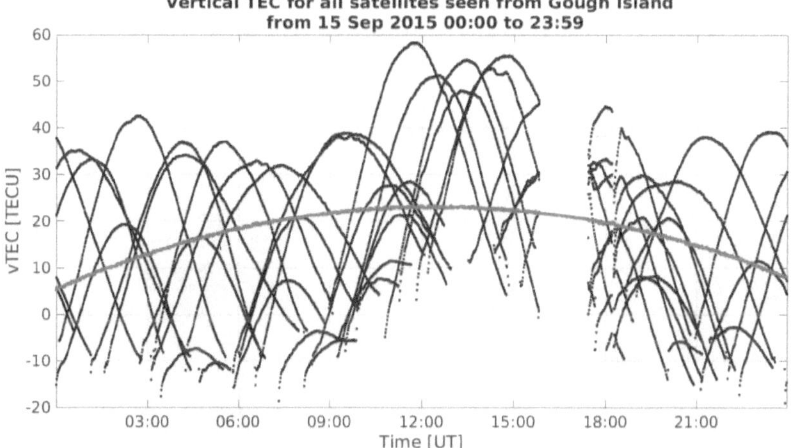

Figure 4.20: Plot ID 31: Examples of typical VTEC graphs are shown here. The data is from 15 September 2015 and is derived from the STEC data from the SA Agulhas II and on Gough Island. The red line is the biased mean VTEC, and the whole plot is offset to place the minimum mean at 5 TECU. The smoothed nature of the VTEC curves allows for more reliable identification of 'ripples' or extreme variations in the VTEC which may be indicators of scintillation. (Top): The SA Agulhas II VTEC ranges between -10 TECU and 60 TECU. No unusual behaviour is visible. (Bottom): The Gough Island VTEC values are negligibly different from the ship values. The Gough Island curves are not as smooth as the ship data, with minor 'rippling' visible just after 09:00 and just before 15:00. The Gough Island VTEC graph has one more curve than the SA Agulhas II graph. The maintenance gap is clearly visible.

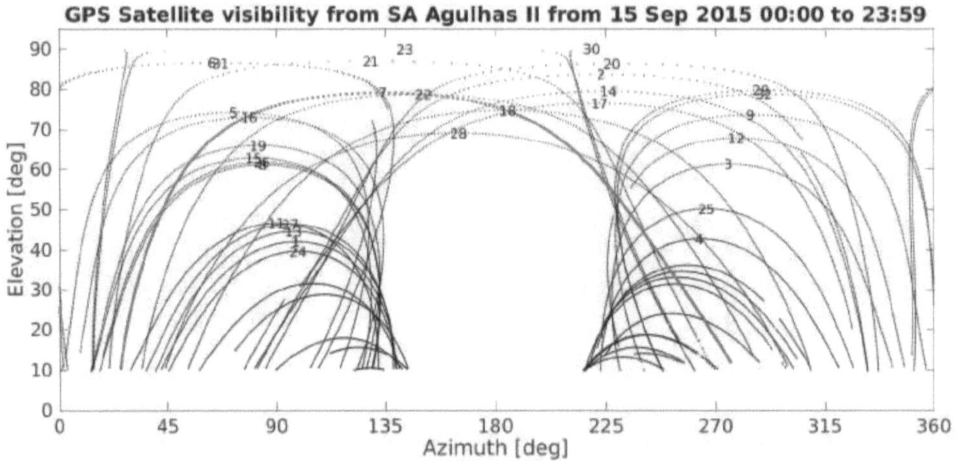

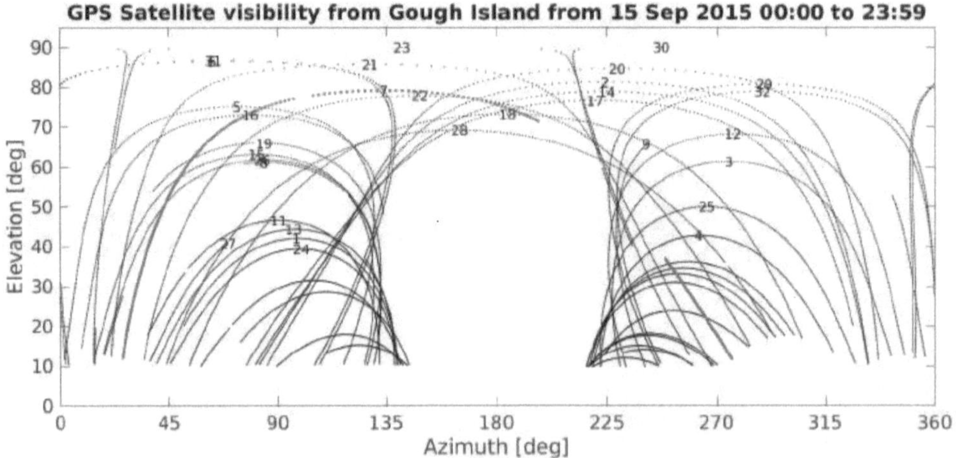

Figure 4.21: Plot ID 50: Examples of GPS satellite visibility tracks for all PRN for a single day (15 September 2015) are shown.. These plots are used to confirm that the same satellites are visible from both receivers. An individual satellite can be highlighted as demonstrated by the red orbital track of PRN 7. (Top): The visibility of the GPS satellites from the SA Agulhas II. There are no obstructions above the 10° minimum elevation to impede the line-of-sight to the GPS satellites. (Bottom): The line-of-sight capability of the fixed GISTM receiver on Gough Island is subject to the geography of the nearby environment; the mountain peaks to the north-west produce a permanent obstruction which spans from roughly 270° to - 330° azimuth and reaches an elevation of almost 20°.

4.5.15   Plot ID 58: Instantaneous Velocity graphs

The graphs shown in Figure 4.22 are examples of the instantaneous velocity of the GISTM antenna of the SA Agulhas II and on Gough Island for a given day. The example data is from 15 September 2015, which is the day on which the SA Agulhas II arrived at Gough Island for the yearly resupply expedition. The ship arrived at its destination at approximately 13:00. The velocity was calculated using the PSN MATLAB script (see Appendix A.2.2) and reflects overall displacement per unit time.

The velocity graphs have a y-axis ranging between 0 and 40 km/h. When the SA Agulhas II is sailing at its average cruising speed, the velocity is expected to be a long segment of positive values with a mean of 24 km/h. When the ship has stopped 'on station' in the ocean to conduct oceanographic research, occasional short-duration spikes are expected as the engines are briefly used to maintain location in response to the natural ocean currents. When drifting without engines, as occurs during marine life observations such as whale-watching or when at anchor just offshore of Gough Island, the velocity readings are expected to be very low but persistent. The Gough Island GISTM is expected to have a velocity of 0 km/h as it is stationary.

The unusual fluctuations observed in multiple σ_ϕ graphs from the SA Agulhas II (see Figures 4.14, 4.15 and 4.16) share a remarkable correlation to the instantaneous velocity of the ship. At 13:00 the ship's velocity decreased from an average of 25 km/h to between 0-1 km/h; at the same time the distribution of the σ_ϕ values narrowed from a range of 5-30 rad to between 2-10 rad. The coinciding changes in σ_ϕ and velocity are visible across all PRN. This is a compelling indicator that the motion of the SA Agulhas II is a dominant contributor of noise to the phase scintillation data recorded by the ship's GISTM.

4.5.16   Plot ID 87: Horizontal Error and Locked Satellites graphs

Figure 4.23 is an example of the horizontal position error and the number of satellites connected for 15 September 2015 from the SA Agulhas II and Gough Island. As the GPS satellites move through the sky, the number of visible space vehicles (SVs) changes. For this research we equate the number of visible satellites to the number of connections the receiver is maintaining.

It is fundamental GPS theory that the more satellites a receiver can access, the higher the accuracy of the position calculation will be. A minimum of 4 GPS satellites is required to determine a location in 3 dimensions (see Section 2.5). The purpose of these graphs is to investigate whether unusual increases in the position error are correlated to a decrease in available GPS satellites or whether they may be a result of severe scintillation.

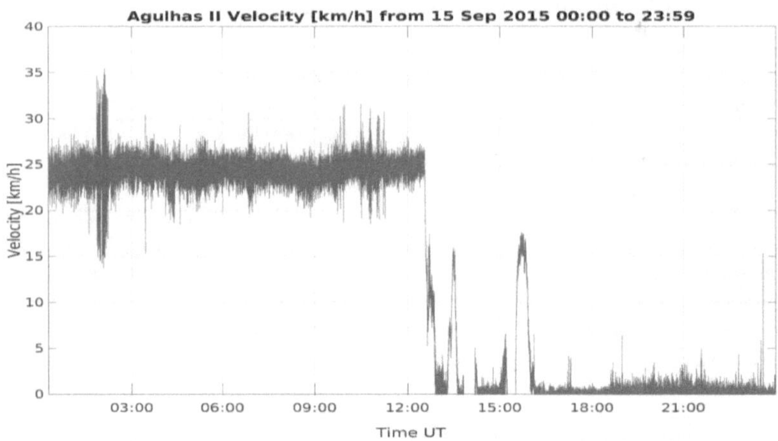

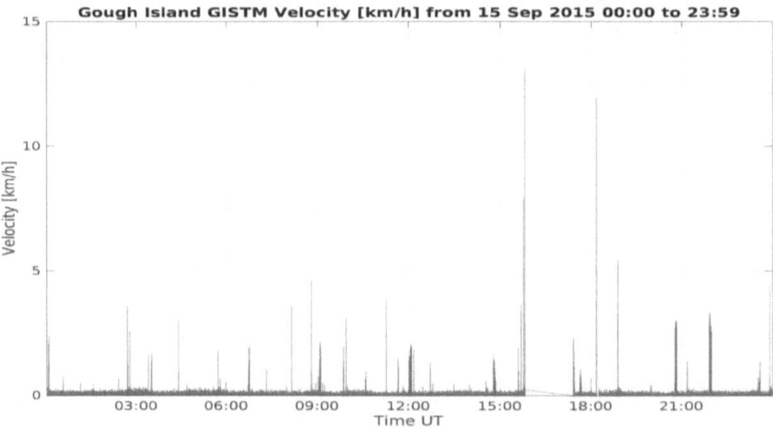

Figure 4.22: Plot ID 58: An example of the instantaneous velocity of the GISTM antenna of the SA Agulhas II and on Gough Island on 15 September 2015 is shown. (Top): The instantaneous velocity of the SA Agulhas II between 00:00 and 13:00 varies from 22-26 km/h but remains continuous, indicating that the ship is sailing at its cruising speed as it approaches Gough Island. An inexplicable symmetric spike occurs at roughly 02:00. At 13:00 the ship arrived at the island and took up a loosely anchored position just offshore, as seen by the drop in velocities to values mostly between 0-1 km/h. Occasional spikes in the velocity are visible as the ship performs minor offshore manoeuvres to find the best position and orientation for helicopter resupply activities to occur. (Bottom): The Gough Island GISTM is stationary yet spikes in the velocity are visible periodically throughout the day. These very short-duration jumps are a result of errors in the position calculations. The maintenance gap is also visible, but with a joining line.

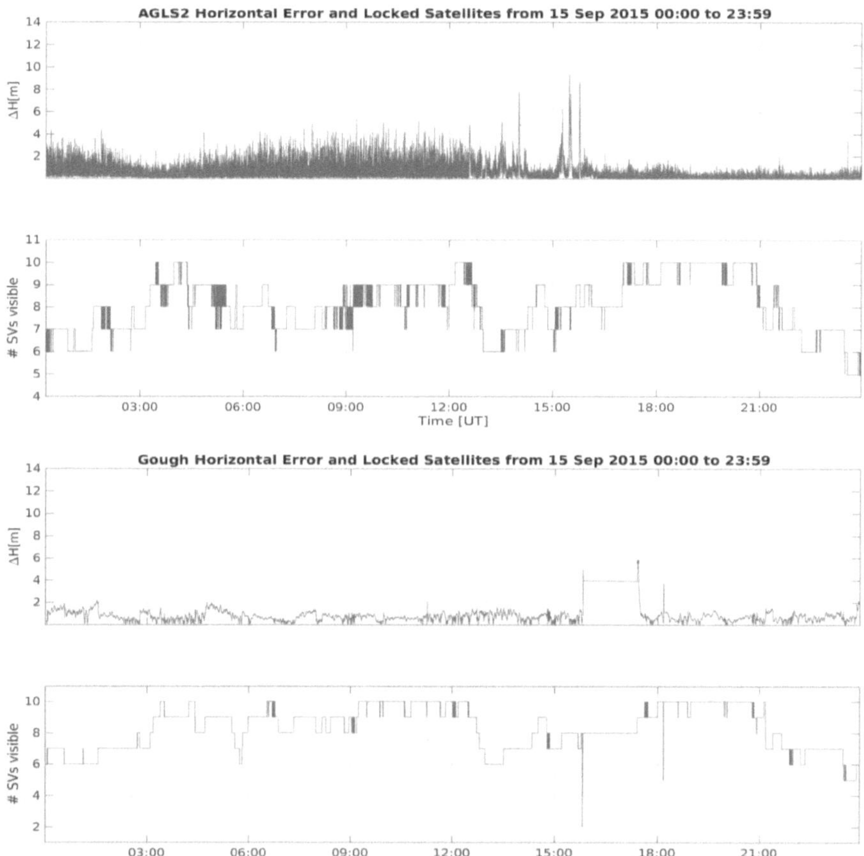

Figure 4.23: Plot ID 87: The horizontal error and simultaneous number of locked GPS satellites (SVs) for 15 September 2015 is shown here. (Top): The number of satellites visible from the SA Agulhas II is generally between 6-10, and drops briefly to 5 near midnight. There are unusual spikes in the horizontal error at 14:00 and again between 15:00-16:00, but no direct correlation to the change in the number of SVs is visible. The horizontal error does show some correlation to the velocity of the ship (see Figure 4.22); the horizontal error is moderate (2-4 m) but fluctuates rapidly until roughly 13:00, then decreases to below 1 m except for a series of strong spikes at times which appear to coincide with sudden increases or decreases in the velocity. (Bottom): The horizontal error from Gough Island is consistently below 2 m, and does not fluctuate rapidly. The number of SVs ranges between 6-10 with a dip to 5 near midnight but is generally higher than the SA Agulhas II values and does not fluctuate nearly as often. The GISTM maintenance is easily visible in the horizontal error but joining lines make it harder to identify in the number of SVs.

4.5.17   Plot ID 88: SA Agulhas II and Gough Island GISTM Trajectory graphs

A plot of the trajectory of the GISTM antennas of the SA Agulhas II and on Gough Island are shown against a large-scale Miller projection map to give context in relation to the SAMA and the surrounding continents. Latitude and Longitude in degrees are used on the axes, and the data is from 15 September 2015. Significant displacement is required for these plots to be particularly useful, and they are best used to map multiple days of data together. Only the SA Agulhas II plots are expected to show any movement. The Gough Island plot is expected to remain as nothing more than a single data point at these scales.

4.5.18   Plot ID 991: Horizontal Position Error Distribution graphs

Figure 4.25 shows an example of the horizontal position error distribution histograms generated for this research. The data shown is from 15 September 2015 as measured from the SA Agulhas II and on Gough Island. The graphs are histograms, and indicate the frequency (y-axis) with which the horizontal position error value (x-axis) fell within a specific range. The bin widths were automatically selected by the MATLAB histogram function to have uniform width while covering the range of x-values in such a way that the shape of the distribution is best displayed. The standard deviation (STD) is calculated for each graph and displayed in the top right corner. The formula used for the horizontal position error is discussed in Section 4.6.

4.5.19   Plot ID 992: Vertical Position Error Distribution graphs

Examples of the vertical position error distribution histograms are shown in Figure 4.26 using data from 15 September 2015 recorded on the SA Agulhas II and on Gough Island. The x-axis shows the vertical error (meters) and the y-axis shows the frequency (counts). The vertical position varies both negatively and positively from the mean value as the ship bobs up and down on the waves. The graph is thus expected to be centred around 0. The STD is displayed in the upper right corner. Bin widths and number of bins are automatically decided by the MATLAB histogram algorithm. The vertical position error is calculated using the difference in height between the recorded value and the mean value.

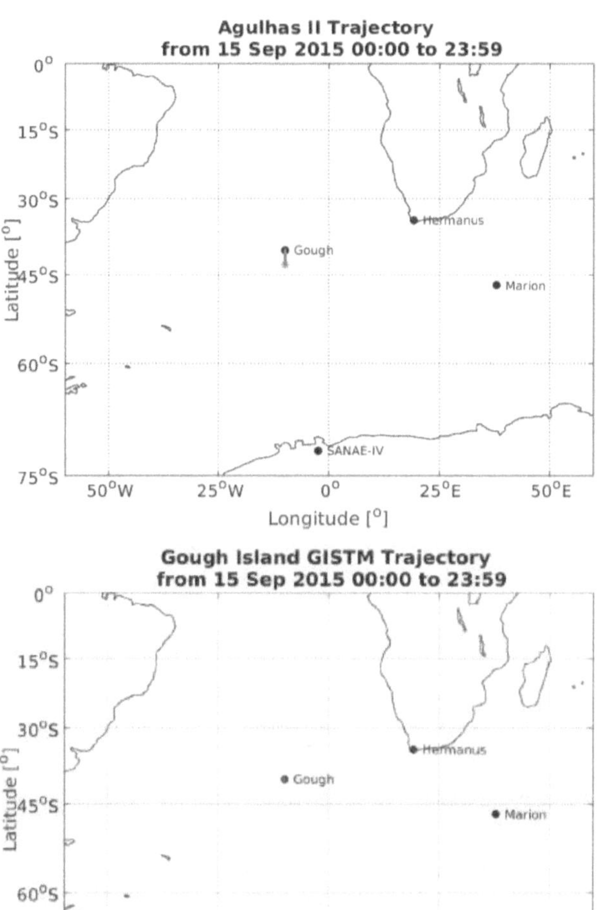

Figure 4.24: Plot ID 88: Examples of the trajectories of the GISTMs on the SA Agulhas II and on Gough Island for 15 September 2015 are shown on a larger map. These maps are well-suited to visualising the displacement of a receiver over larger distances. (Top): The SA Agulhas II approached Gough Island from the south (trajectory begins at the star) and was still at the island at the end of the day. (Bottom): The GISTM on Gough Island is stationary, and it is not unexpected to see that the position remained unchanged the whole day.

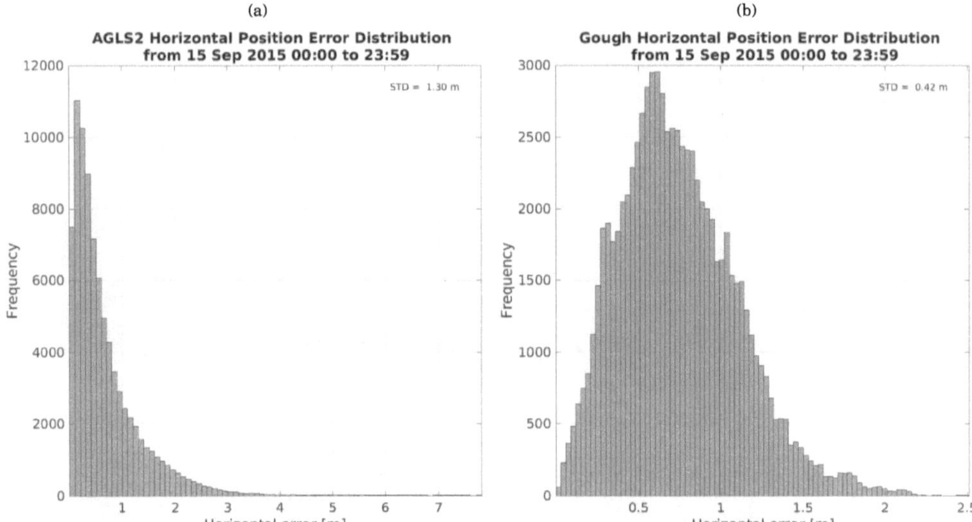

Figure 4.25: Plot ID 991: The horizontal position error distribution is shown for 15 September 2015 from the SA Agulhas II and on Gough Island. (a): The SA Agulhas II had an STD of 1.30 m, a maximum count of 11000 for 0.1-0.2 m horizontal error, and the tail of the distribution reaches negligible count values at 4 m. The maximum horizontal error recorded was between 7.7-7.8 m. (b): Gough Island had significantly smaller error values and counts than the ship; the STD was 0.42 m, the maximum count was roughly 2900 for 0.59-0.62 m as well as 0.62-0.65 m, the tail values are negligible at 2.2 m, and the maximum horizontal error recorded was 205 m. The Gough Island horizontal position error is therefore much lower than the SA Agulhas II horizontal position error.

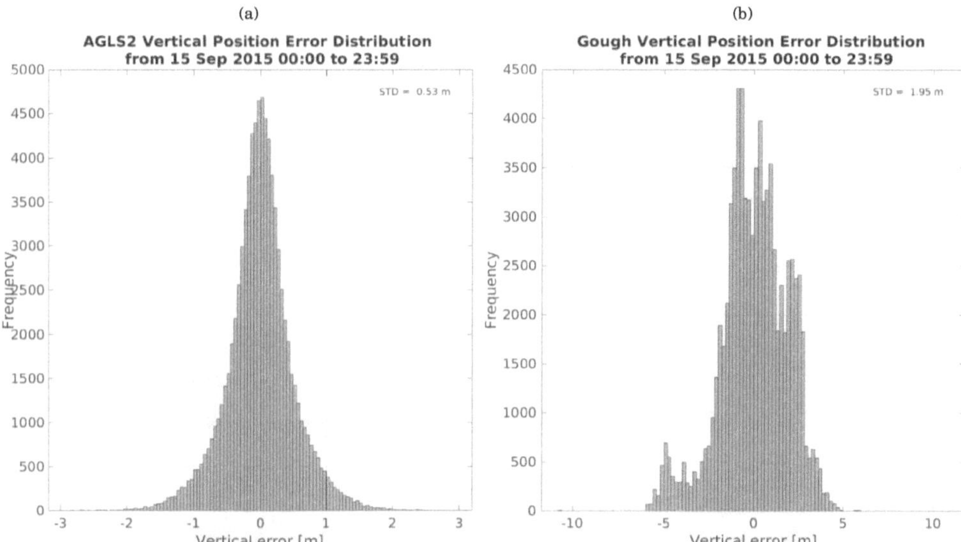

Figure 4.26: Plot ID 992: Examples of the vertical position error distribution histograms are shown here, using data from 15 September 2015. (a): The STD of the SA Agulhas II is 0.53 m, with a maximum count of 4700 centred around 0 m. The symmetric tail values reach negligible counts at 2 m, and the maximum vertical errors recorded are ±3.2 m. (b): Surprisingly, the Gough Island vertical position errors are up to three times higher than those of the SA Agulhas II, with only slightly lower counts. The STD for Gough Island is 1.95 m, however the distribution is not symmetrical, and the highest counts are observed at roughly -2 m and 0.5 m. The maximum vertical errors recorded are approximately ±13 m. The magnitude of these error values, as well as the shape of this error distribution, are unusual.

4.5.20 Plot ID 993: Absolute Position Error Distribution graphs

The absolute position error distribution histograms for the SA Agulhas II and on Gough Island on 15 September 2015 are shown in Figure 4.27 as examples of this graph. The vertical position error is a combination of the horizontal and vertical components seen in Figures 4.25 and 4.26. The absolute position error is a positive value. The STD is calculated and displayed in the upper right corner. As with a typical histogram, the magnitude is on the x-axis (error in meters) and the frequency (count values) are on the y-axis. The bin configuration is determined by MATLAB within the histogram function.

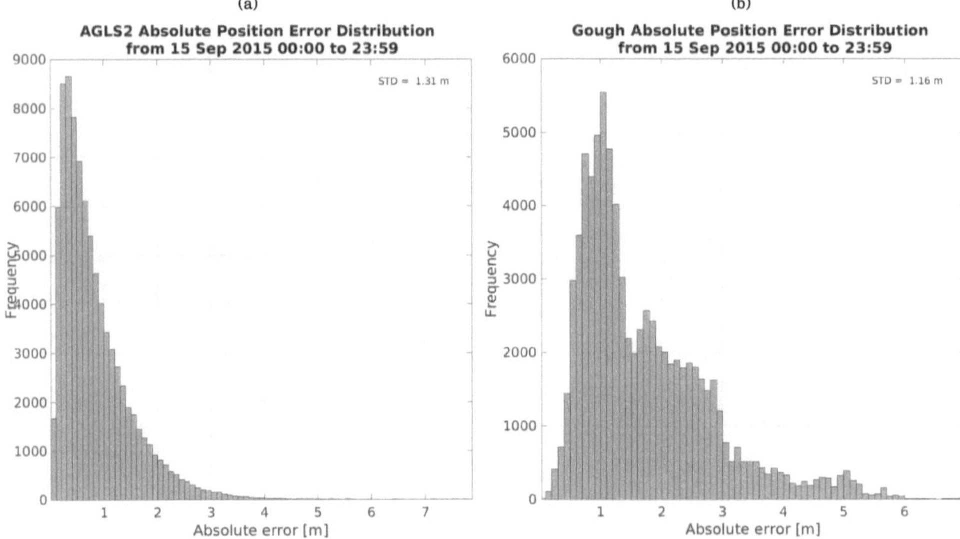

Figure 4.27: Plot ID 993: An example of the absolute position error distribution histograms used in this research are shown here, using data from 15 September 2015. (a): The STD of the SA Agulhas II is 1.31 m, with maximum counts of 8700 at 0.3-0.4 m and 8500 at 0.2-0.3 m. The tail values reach negligible counts at 4 m, and the maximum vertical errors recorded are ±7.8 m. (b): The Gough Island absolute position errors are on the same order of magnitude as the SA Agulhas II, but while the counts are somewhat lower the magnitudes of the errors do not drop off as fast. The distribution is not a smooth curve. The STD for Gough Island is 1.16 m, and the count values only drop to negligible amounts at 6 m. The maximum vertical errors recorded are ±7 m. The persistent higher counts for higher magnitude error values, as well as the shape of the absolute position error distribution is odd.

4.5.21   Plot ID 994: Variation in Latitude, Longitude and Altitude graphs

The example graph of the change in coordinates for the SA Agulhas II and Gough Island are shown in Figure 4.28. These 3-pane graphs serve to provide clarification on any irregularities observed in the horizontal and vertical component position error distribution graphs discussed in Sections 4.25 and 4.26. The coordinates are measured in degrees, with latitude in the top pane and longitude in the middle pane. The altitude of the antenna is measured in meters above sea level and displayed in the bottom pane.

4.5.22   Plot ID 995: Running Mean Error graphs

Figure 4.29 is a different way to view the same information seen in the coordinate change graphs from Section 4.5.21. This 3-pane example demonstrates the variation from the mean of the absolute (ΔR), horizontal (ΔH) and vertical (Δh) values measured in meters. The middle pane, ΔH, is the same graph as the one used in the comparison with the number of locked satellites in Figure 4.23. ΔR is a positive value made up from the ΔH and Δh components.

4.5.23   Plot ID 996: Latitude-Longitude Scatter Plot

Figure 4.30 presents examples of latitude-longitude position estimates scatter plots for 15 September 2015 as recorded from the SA Agulhas II and on Gough Island. These plots are meant to provide additional context to (and a slightly different view of the data from) the various PSN plots discussed thus far. It is important to note that the scatter plots are formatted to be square, but the axes are scaled to fit the recorded latitude and longitude values and as a result the ranges displayed on the two axes are likely to be different. The scatter plots are a useful tool for identifying the 20 largest outlying values and highlighting them in relation to the rest of the plot.

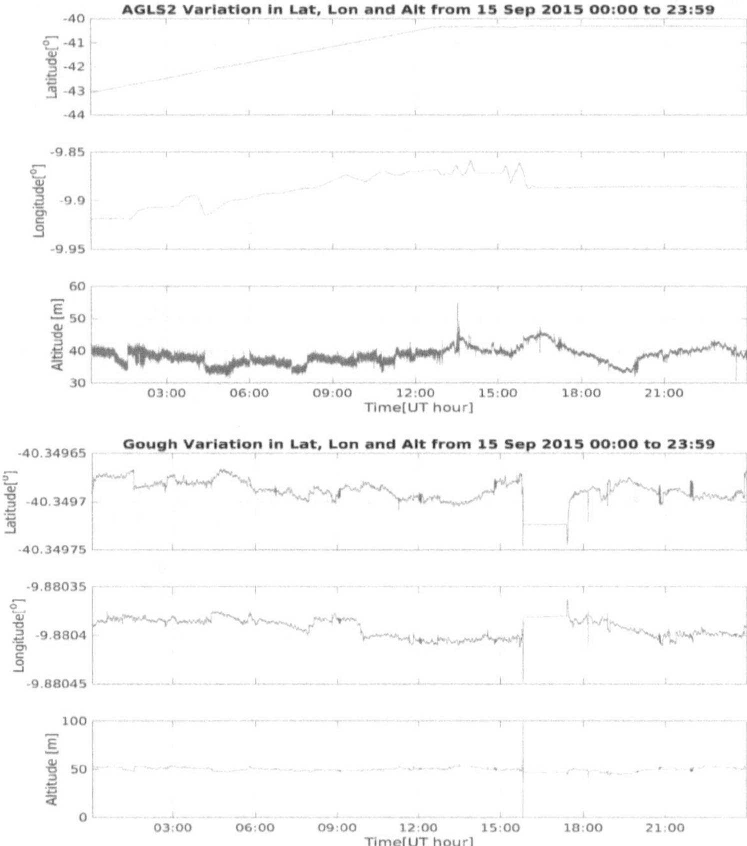

Figure 4.28: Plot ID 994: The variation in latitude, longitude and altitude for the SA Agulhas II and on Gough Island measured on 15 September 2015 are shown in this 3-pane graph. (Top): The SA Agulhas II was sailing northwards until 13:00; the large increase in latitude with the small change in longitude confirms this trajectory. After 13:00, the ship remains local, with only minor variations in longitude as the best location for resupply operations is found. The altitude oscillates rapidly until 13:00 but remains within the small range of 35–40 m above sea level. After 13:00 the magnitude of the rapid oscillations is decreased. At 13:30 a large spike in the altitude is observed which coincides with the first velocity spike after 13:00 in Figure 4.22, as well as with the longitude variations. (Bottom): By comparison, the Gough Island coordinate variations are minuscule and the fluctuations occur much slower. The altitude remains consistent at 50 m except for a ±50 m symmetrical spike which coincides with the start of the GISTM maintenance period. This anomalous data point has skewed the Gough Island vertical position error distribution in Figure 4.26.

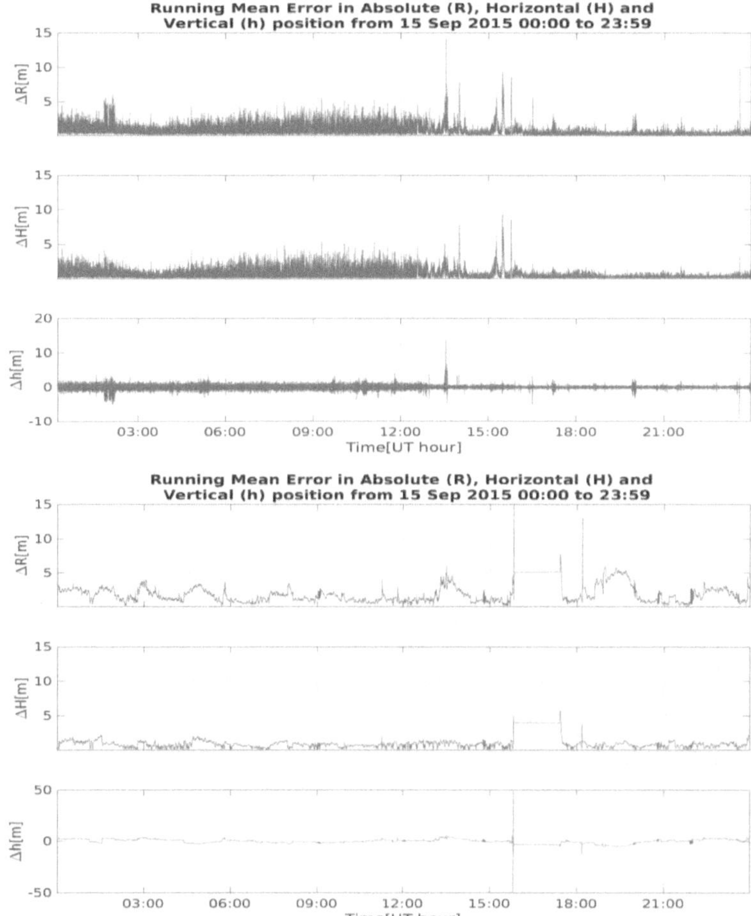

Figure 4.29: Plot ID 995: These 3-pane graphs show the running mean error in ΔR (top), ΔH (middle) and Δh (bottom) for 15 September 2015 from the SA Agulhas II and on Gough Island. The mean as well as the error values are directly derived from the coordinate and altitude variations shown in Figure 4.28 and thus display related features. (Top): The SA Agulhas II errors are larger and fluctuate more rapidly than the Gough Island errors. After 13:00, the magnitude of the errors decrease as the ship is no longer sailing at high velocity. (Bottom): The Gough Island errors are on the same order of magnitude as the ship, however the intensity of the fluctuations are lower. The Δh values match the variation in altitude from Figure 4.28. The GISTM power losses are also clearly visible, and the large spike in Δh is directly correlated with the start of the maintenance work.

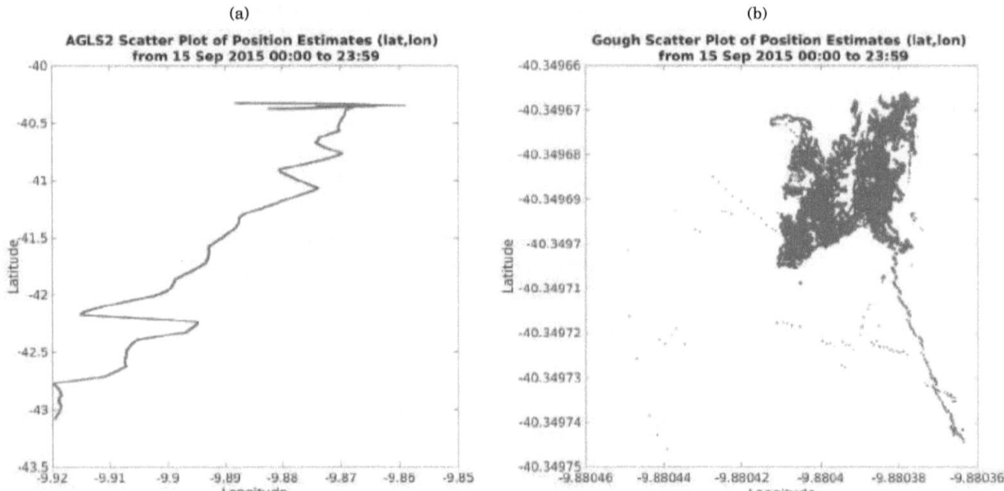

Figure 4.30: Plot ID 996: Examples of latitude-longitude scatter plots of position estimates for the SA Agulhas II and on Gough Island drawn for 15 September 2015. (a): The SA Agulhas II latitude values range between -43.1° and -40.3°. The longitude values range between -9.92° and -9.859°. The SA Agulhas II is a moving platform; the coordinates are expected to cover a wide range of values depending on the magnitude of the ship's motion. (b): The Gough Island latitude values range between -40.349745° and -40.349667°. The longitude values range between -9.88045° and -9.880364°. The Gough Island antenna is stationary and the position estimates are expected to be very precise with a small variance. The immense difference in the order of magnitude of values data plotted on the SA Agulhas II graph against the Gough Island graph confirms that the GISTM on the island is stationary relative to the motion of the ship.

4.5.24 Plot ID 997: X-Y Position Estimate Scatter Plot

The data used to generate the scatter plots depicted in Figure 4.31 is directly derived from the coordinate data shown in Figure 4.30. The X-Y values (measured in the more human-friendly unit of meters) are presented in the form of a deviation from the mean position (0,0) which is indicated on the plot by the red triangle. The STD is indicated by the red circle around the zero position. The x-axis shows 'dLon' (East-West variations) and the y-axis shows 'dLat' (north-south variations).

For the moving case of the SA Agulhas II, the deviation is calculated from the running mean centred over a 60-second window, which is why the values on the y-axis do not exceed 100 m despite the ship travelling nearly 100 km in the first half of the day. Calculated over such short intervals, the ship's new current position will not be very far from the mean position. The Gough Island GISTM mean position is calculated using deviations from the true, fixed location. The STD is shown in the upper right corner.

This is the last plot type example as generated using the MATLAB code. These sets of graphs were run for single days and combinations of days over the period 15-28 September 2015. The results of the analysis of these graphs are discussed in Chapter 5.

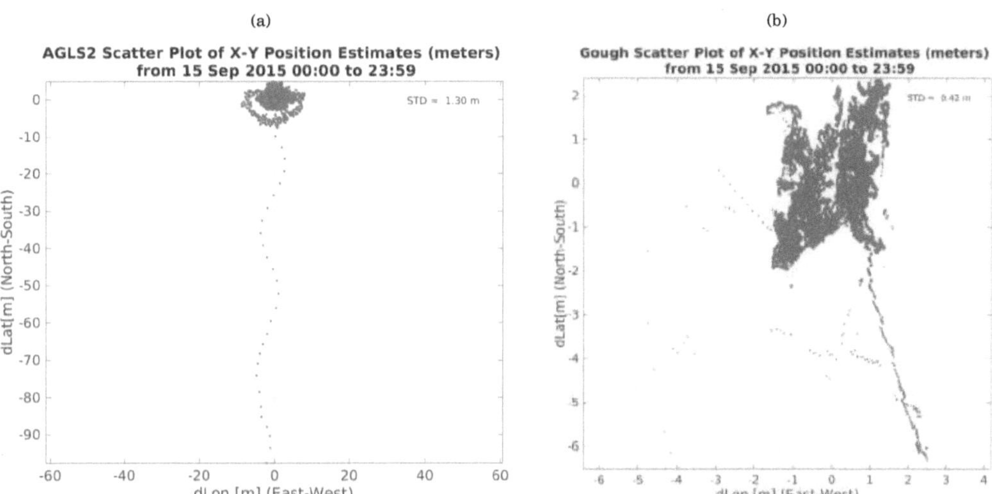

Figure 4.31: Plot ID 997: Examples of latitude-longitude scatter plots of position estimates for the SA Agulhas II and Gough Island drawn for 15 September 2015. (a): The SA Agulhas II GISTM latitude variations range between -43.1° and -40.3°. The longitude variations range between -9.92° and -9.859°. The SA Agulhas II is a moving platform; the GISTM antenna coordinate variations are expected to cover a wide range of values depending on the magnitude of the ship's motion. (b): The Gough Island GISTM latitude variations range between -40.349745° and -40.349667°. The longitude values range between -9.88045° and -9.880364°. The Gough Island GISTM antenna is stationary and the position estimates are expected to be very precise with a small variance. The immense difference in the order of magnitude of the variations plotted on the SA Agulhas II graph compared to the Gough Island graph confirms that the GISTM on the island is stationary relative to the motion of the GISTM on the ship.

4.6 Calculation of position accuracy

The error in the position estimate of a GISTM receiver is an important parameter to assess the potential impact of ionospheric scintillation. The SA Agulhas II, however, is perpetually in motion during voyages, even when paused 'on-station' to conduct oceanographic experiments.

To calculate the position error, the difference between the recorded value and the mean value is normally used for a stationary receiver. Geographically, the mean receiver position is a central location which most accurately describes the true position of the receiver. The accuracy is determined by the latitude and longitude differences from those central coordinates.

Due to the constantly changing position of the SA Agulhas II GISTM receiver, a new algorithm was needed to calculate the error in the recorded position. The SA Agulhas II position error was defined as the instantaneous GPS receiver position minus the mean GPS receiver position. However, a ship in linear motion has no mean GPS receiver position because there is a constant change in the true GPS receiver coordinates, resulting in a 'mean path' rather than a fixed point mean.

Calculating the GPS position accuracy for a continually moving target therefore requires the use of a running mean algorithm. This segments the overall motion into a series of positional snapshots instead. The mean position varies as it moves over time, and is relative to the prior and subsequent positions. The time over which the running mean is calculated must be balanced with the number of data points available within that window.

A smaller window provides more accurate variance calculations, but has fewer data points, making the result less statistically significant. A larger window allows for a greater overall movement of the ship, and the variances calculated will thus be greater, artificially introducing error. The selected window for this book was a period of 60 seconds, centred on the time of comparison.

Since movement is a combination of latitude and longitude changes, one way to increase the accuracy of the position variance calculation is to address each axis independently and then recombine the results. A graphic illustrating the mean path and error calculation for a single axis is shown in Figure 4.32. The running means were calculated separately for the latitude and longitude using a series of 60 second windows over a whole day which were then combined to determine the position errors the SA Agulhas II GPS receiver.

The use of the running mean is only valid for a moving receiver. The position error of the Gough Island GISTM was calculated normally as the true position of the receiver is known.

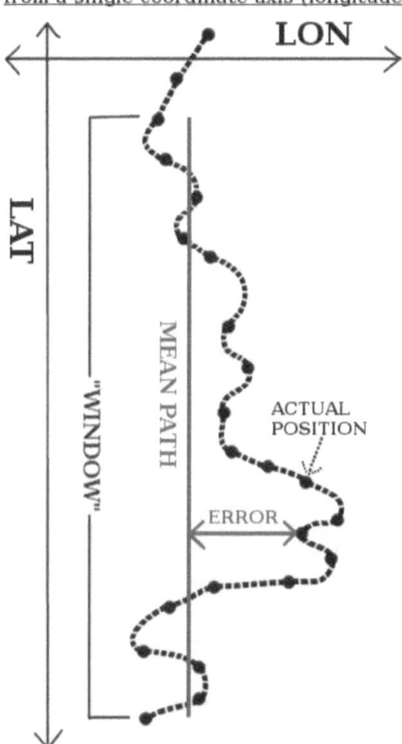

Figure 4.32: Graphic depicting the single-axis running mean position accuracy algorithm. The mean path is calculated using the longitude position values over a selected time window. The position error is the difference between the mean path and the actual position, for the centre value of the shifting window.

4.7   Filtering of Motion Noise

The motion noise in the scintillation data from the SA Agulhas II is clearly visible when compared to the same scintillation data from Gough Island. The S_4 values measured from the ship tend to be 1-3 times larger than their stationary counterparts, and more widely distributed. The σ_ϕ values from the SA Agulhas II can be as high as300 times larger than the Gough Island data and also exhibit a very wide distribution. Only the σ_ϕ values appear artificially amplified but this behaviour is not unexpected; the power of the recorded signal (S_4) is not affected by the movement of the ship.

Noise is a well-studied phenomenon; many methods can be used to filter it out. Attempting to remove noise from a data set, however, without an idea of the characteristics of the noise itself may produce a smoothed result, but does not necessarily result in scientifically valuable data. A likely source for this noise (movement) is known and can aid in developing an appropriate filter. The noise may have a single source or be a result of a combination of sources. These factors affect the type of filter used. The characteristics of the data set must also be considered.

Different types of motion are experienced by the SA Agulhas II: translation, axial movements, and vibration (see Section 3.3). The translation motion can be interpreted as the distance the ship has sailed from its starting point; this tends to be a linearly increasing value over long periods. The σ_ϕ noise appears to be correlated to the velocity of the ship, which is the rate of change of the distance over time.

Of the axial movements, the side-to-side rolling motion (around the x-axis) can displace the antenna the most. The tolerance of the system to errors introduced because of this rolling motion has already been established (see Section 3.3) and is not expected to produce any noise or errors in the data. The receiver and antenna are physically located very close to the midpoint of the ship with regards to the pitch (y) and yaw (z) axes; any slewing or pitching of the ship around these two axes will have a minimal effect on the position of the antenna.

The two remaining motion types are the up-down motion (bobbing) of the ship as effected by waves, and the vibrations through the superstructure resulting from machinery and impacts with the ocean surface (slamming) or onto ice (to break through). Data for the vibration of the ship could be obtained from a vibration sensor network belonging to a research team from Stellenbosch University, however it was decided that vibration analysis falls outside the scope of this research.

A random 2-hour sample of PSN data was selected from the SA Agulhas II data files to use in the analysis of the vertical motion. A plot of the typical vertical displacement of the antenna (height above sea level) over an excerpt of 5 minutes is shown in Figure 4.33. The periodicity of the vertical motion is clearly visible and has to correlate to a dominant frequency. The Period04 software package (Lenz and Breger, 2010) was used to perform a frequency analysis using Fourier transforms.

The result of the SA Agulhas II vertical frequency response analysis is shown in Figure 4.34. The analysis was constrained to frequencies between 0.001 Hz and 0.22 Hz for greatest clarity in the results. The dominant frequency peak is visible at 0.1 Hz. Since the PSN files are sampled once per second (1 Hz), only frequencies of up to the Nyquist Frequency of 0.5 Hz can be detected using the antenna height data. Even the vibration frequencies for the SA Agulhas II are expected to be higher than this. Retroactively filtering the noise out of such low time resolution data is thus not possible.

High time-resolution scintillation data is available in the NVD files recorded by the SA Agulhas II GISTM (See Section 3.4.1). The sample rate of the NVD data is 50 Hz, allowing for analysis of frequencies up to 25 Hz. This maximum frequency is 50 times higher than the maximum frequency that can be observed in the PSN data. Unfortunately the NVD binary file does not contain any position information and would require significant processing before the raw data it contains could be used. This exercise was

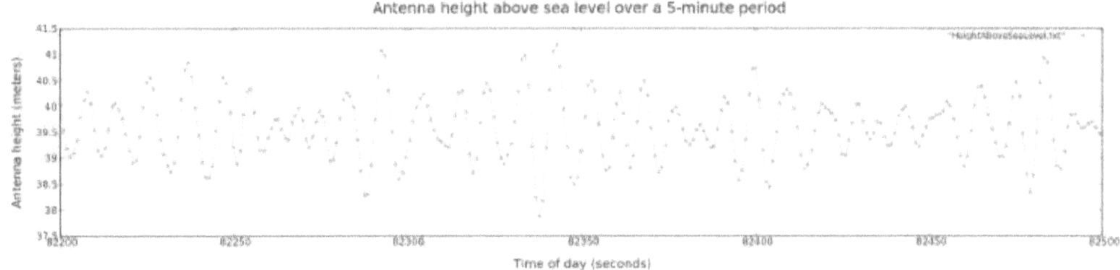

Figure 4.33: A graph of the vertical displacement of the GISTM antenna on the SA Agulhas II over a randomly selected 5-minute excerpt of the 2-hour PSN data sample shows the clear cyclic pattern of the motion.

deemed to be beyond the scope of this research.

The monitoring of ionospheric scintillation from ocean-based platforms is not a novel concept. Research has been conducted by Atmospheric & Space Technology Research Associates (ASTRA) using buoys and ocean gliders sent out to sea carrying a specially designed receiver called the GPS Autonomous Micro-Monitor at ASTRA (GAMMA). Significant noise was observed by ASTRA in both the phase scintillation measurements (σ_ϕ) and the VTEC as a result of the moving platform (Azeem et al., 2015).

The GAMMA has a high raw data rate of 100 Hz. A series of proprietary algorithms were developed by ASTRA which make use of satellite geometry, antenna movement direction, and the change in the integrated carrier phase to subtract the effect of the antenna movement from the observations in real-time. Multiple field tests of the GAMMA and the algorithms have resulted in high accuracy results despite the movement of the platform. ASTRA is a commercial entity and the GAMMA unit can be purchased (Azeem et al., 2016).

It became clear that the motion noise in the the SA Agulhas II scintillation data would overwhelm any potential ionospheric scintillation events, making it unlikely that scintillation could be identified in this research. Filtering the noise out was not possible and thus the decision was made to focus instead on characterising the possible effects of scintillation and movement on the various parameters recorded by the GISTM. The corresponding scintillation and position data from the Gough Island GISTM was used as the control.

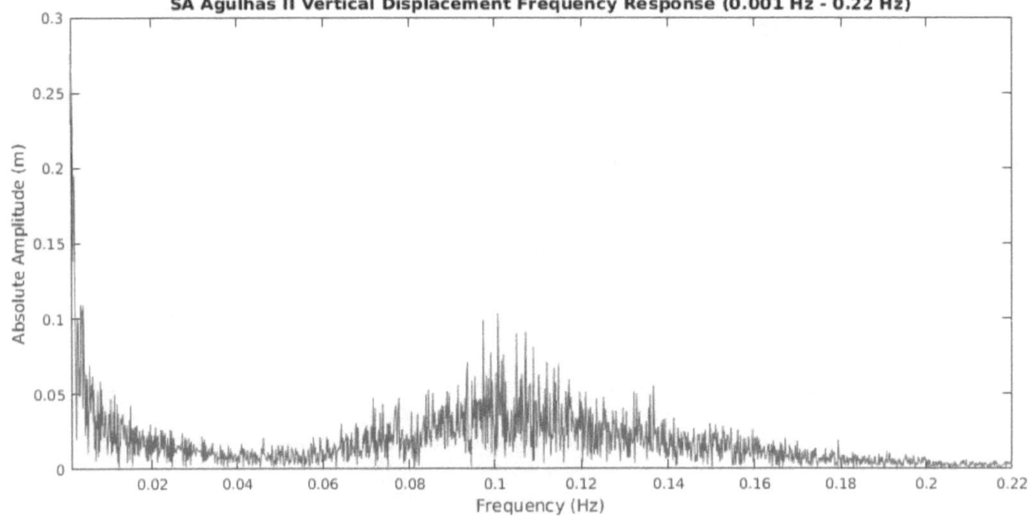

Figure 4.34: The vertical displacement frequency response of the SA Agulhas II between 0.001 Hz and 0.22 Hz is shown here. The peak response at 0.1 Hz indicates the dominant frequency observed in the 1 Hz antenna height data. The sampling rate is too low to provide a proper frequency spectrum analysis which can be used to develop or select a filter to remove the motion noise effect.

CHAPTER

5

RESULTS AND DISCUSSION

In this chapter the results of data analysis are discussed. A brief summary of the findings from the scintillation count histograms is provided, including the outcomes of the data correction process. The hypothesis that the movement of the SA Agulhas II generates noise in the scintillation data is tested and shown to be correct.

The motion noise effect is discussed and the Gough data is analysed to determine the presence of scintillation. The SYM-H index is used to determine the geomagnetic storm conditions. A brief comparison of scintillation during storm times is conducted with a GISTM station outside the SAMA.

5.1 Daily scintillation count histograms

The daily scintillation count histograms are used to measure the number of events in which the threshold value of 0.2 for both S_4 (dimensionless) and σ_ϕ (radians) were exceeded. The histograms were used as a first-look mechanism to test the fidelity of the SA Agulhas II's GISTM data while also providing a visual overview of the scintillation data recorded thus far. The problems identified in the operation of the GISTM, the incongruities in the data, and the process developed to correct the issues are discussed in Section 3.5. Additional details and code used in the corrections are available in Appendix A.

The resulting correction programs and rectified data could then be used for proper scientific analysis. Additionally, the SANSA engineering team was able to use the details of the correction process to apply fixes to the GISTM on the SA Agulhas II, ensuring an accurate system configuration for the recording of subsequent data.

Excessive σ_ϕ scintillation counts and fluctuations well above the typical values seen with stationary receivers were observed across the entire data set. A comparison with corresponding data from the nearest fixed GISTM in Hermanus is detailed in Section 4.2. The results of this comparison provided the basis for the motion-induced scintillation noise hypothesis; it was unlikely that the variations were due to precipitation events.

Further analysis of the scintillation count histograms and the movement of the ship over a longer period was conducted to determine the validity of the motion-noise hypothesis. The results are shown in Section 4.2.1 and gave strong credence to the idea that the presence of scintillation events would be masked by the high levels of motion-induced noise. Scintillation data was obtained from Gough Island, located within the South Atlantic Magnetic Anomaly (SAMA), and subjected to multiple constraints to ensure the legitimacy of a comparison with the SA Agulhas II scintillation data. The outcomes can be reviewed in Sections 4.3 and 4.4.

A frequency spectrum analysis was performed on the SA Agulhas II vertical position data in order to identify dominant frequencies which might be related to the motion and thus allow for filtering out the motion-induced noise (see Section 4.7). It was determined that the 1-second time resolution of the position data was not suffiecient to allow filtering of the expected vibration frequencies of the SA Agulhas II. The research then moved on to a detailed analysis of the parameters recorded by the GISTMs on the SA Agulhas II and on Gough Island. The details of this analysis are covered by Section 5.2 and examples of each of the plots generated are available in Section 4.5.

5.2   Motion-induced scintillation noise

The hypothesis of the noise in the scintillation data being due to the motion of the SA Agulhas II was then investigated by overlaying the velocity data with the σ_ϕ data. Figures 5.1 and 5.2 show the results of such an overlay for 15, 25 and 28 September 2015. The corrected σ_ϕ is shown on the left axis in red, and the absolute value of the antenna velocity (V_a) is shown on the right axis in blue.

The concurrent behaviour of the two parameters was observed repeatedly throughout the ship's visit to the island, providing indisputable evidence of a correlation between antenna velocity and phase scintillation.

The absolute value of the velocity measurement was used in these plots as the direction of the ship's motion had no effect on the noise levels introduced to the scintillation data. The intensity and duration of the velocity appear to have a greater effect on the distribution and fluctuations of the σ_ϕ than on the S_4.

Not every spike in the velocity shows an associated change in the scintillation; short-duration changes in velocity are easily visible as they are plotted from 1-second PSN data while the phase scintillation index is plotted using 50 Hz ISM data statistics averaged over 1 minute by the GPS-SCINDA software. The difference in time resolution may result in some features of the velocity variation being obscured in the σ_ϕ data.

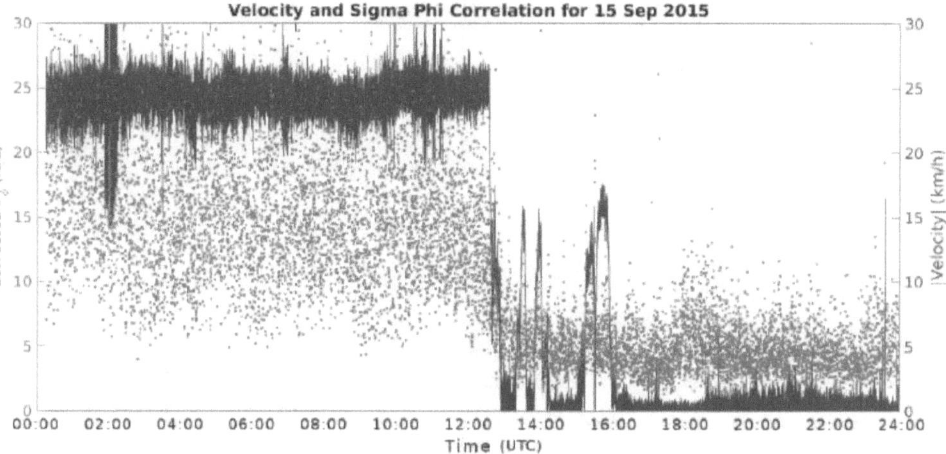

Figure 5.1: The SA Agulhas II velocity data was combined with the corrected σ_ϕ data. On 15 September 2015, the SA Agulhas II arrived at Gough Island's Quest Bay at approximately 13:00 UTC. The velocity drops from an average of 24 km/h to between 1-3 km/h. The distribution of σ_ϕ values concurrently change from a wide distribution (5-30 rad) to a narrower range (2-10 rad).

5.3 Gough Island scintillation observations

It was determined that the motion-induced noise in the SA Agulhas II scintillation data would effectively mask any actual scintillation events from being observed. However, the absence of proof of scintillation is not proof of the absence of scintillation. The stationary GISTM receiver on Gough Island is not subject to the same motion effects as the SA Agulhas II; the S_4 and σ_ϕ data recorded from the island for the period 15-28 September 2015, when the SA Agulhas II was within 100km of Gough Island, were inspected to determine whether scintillation actually occurred.

The Gough Island histograms showed only a single count of $S_4 > 0.5$, on 23 September 2015, and only 20 counts above 0.2 were recorded that day, even though $S_4 > 0.5$ scintillation levels were observed at SANAE-IV on 20 September 2015 (see Section 5.4). A single data point is not sufficient evidence to conclude that scintillation actually took place; it is more likely to be an aberrant reading. It was determined that significant scintillations ($S_4 > 0.4$) were not detected at Gough Island during the SA Agulhas II's visit.

5.4 SYM-H geomagnetic storm index

The SYM-H index records for the period 15-28 September 2015 were obtained as in some regions scintillation is enhanced by the presence of geomagnetic storm conditions (Kyoto Geomagnetic World Data Centre,

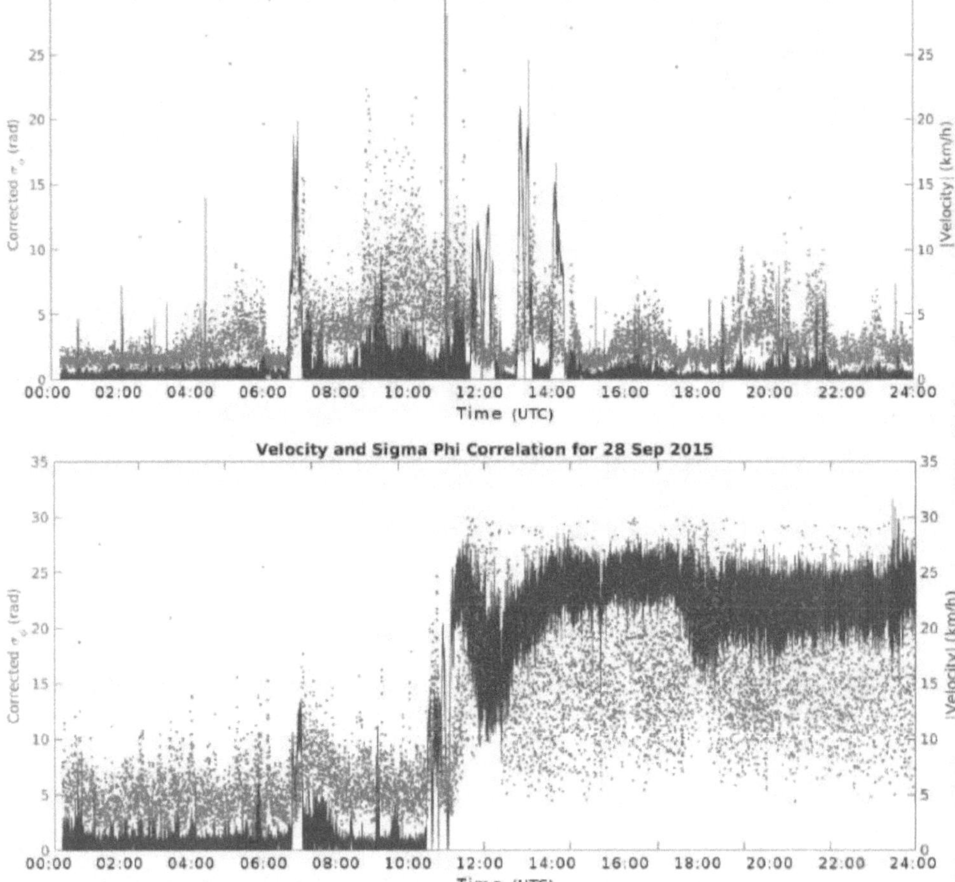

Figure 5.2: The SA Agulhas II velocity data overlaid with the corrected σ_ϕ data. (Top): On 25 September 2015, the SA Agulhas II sailed back and forth along the eastern and north-eastern coast of Gough Island between four different anchor locations; these movements present as peaks in the velocity, with periods of slow drift bracketed by occasional small spikes associated with strong engine thrust action to maintain a stationary position. The pattern of the σ_ϕ values is uncanny in its shadowing of the velocity graph. (Bottom): On 28 September 2015 the SA Agulhas II actively maintained its position for final helicopter loading activities using slow but sustained engine thrust. At 11:00 the ship sail northwards from the island, accelerating to its average cruising velocity of 24 km/h. The σ_ϕ distribution remains between 2.5-10 rad until 11:00 and then increases to a range of 5-30 rad.

2015). Figure 5.3 reveals a storm which occurred on 20 September 2015; A single day view shows the SYM-H index dropping to -75 nT ('moderate') at 11:00. It is likely that scintillation would take place at this time.

The SYM-H is a high-resolution global geomagnetic storm index (Wanliss and Showalter, 2006); a check for any scintillation which may have been recorded close to but outside the SAMA region during the storm period was merited (see Section 2.9). The SANAE IV base in Vesleskarvet, Antarctica, produces a monthly space weather report; the storm conditions seen in the SYM-H were also recorded by the SANAE-IV GISTM. The report indicated a class M2 solar flare ('moderate') on 20 September 2015, with a planetary K-Index of 7 ('strong') resulting in σ_ϕ values of 0.3 being exceeded 77 times (Lilla and Potgieter, 2015).

Figure 5.4 shows that there were also 23 counts of σ_ϕ above 0.4 and 2 events where S_4 rose above 0.5 from SANAE IV. More than 50 of these counts took place within a 10-minute period. The corresponding graph from Gough Island shows barely any activity in comparison. The corrected S_4 from 20 September 2015 for Gough Island as seen in Figure 5.5 (combined with the SA Agulhas II S_4 data) shows no trace of scintillation activity beyond the background levels observed at Gough Island.

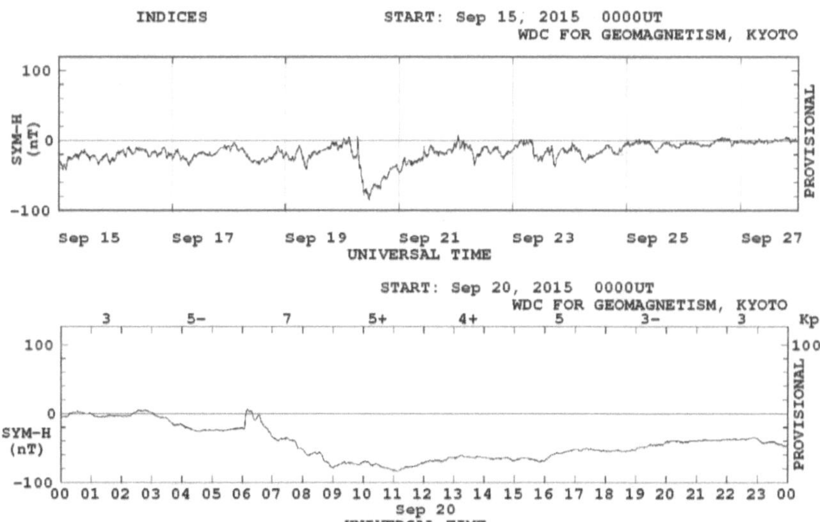

Figure 5.3: (Top): The global SYM-H index for the period 15-28 September 2015 is shown. A large fluctuation indicating a storm is visible on 20 September 2015. (Bottom): The detailed graph of the SYM-H index for 20 September 2015 shows a highly typical geomagnetic storm profile reaching a minimum of -75 nT at 11:00.

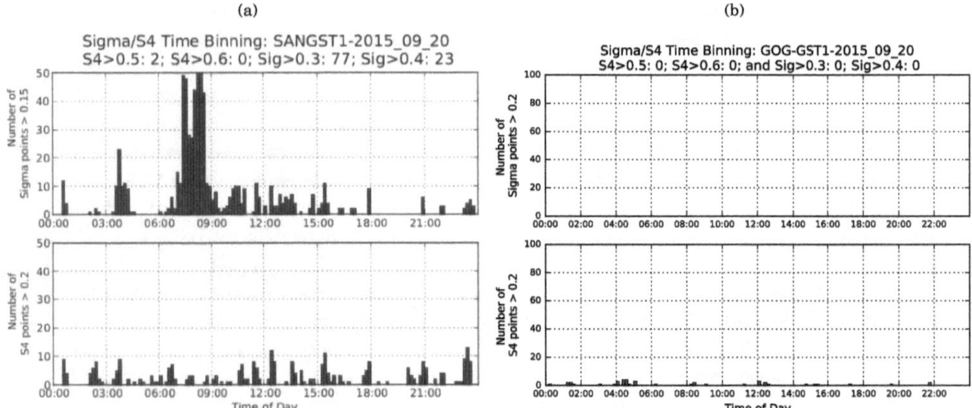

Figure 5.4: The scintillation count histograms from SANAE IV and Gough Island for 20 September 2015 are shown here. (a): SANAE IV recorded significant activity in both σ_ϕ and S_4, with 77 counts above 0.3 rad. The σ_ϕ activity occurred predominantly between 07:00-09:00. (b): No significant scintillation was recorded on Gough Island, showing that the geomagnetic storm effect did not extend into the SAMA.

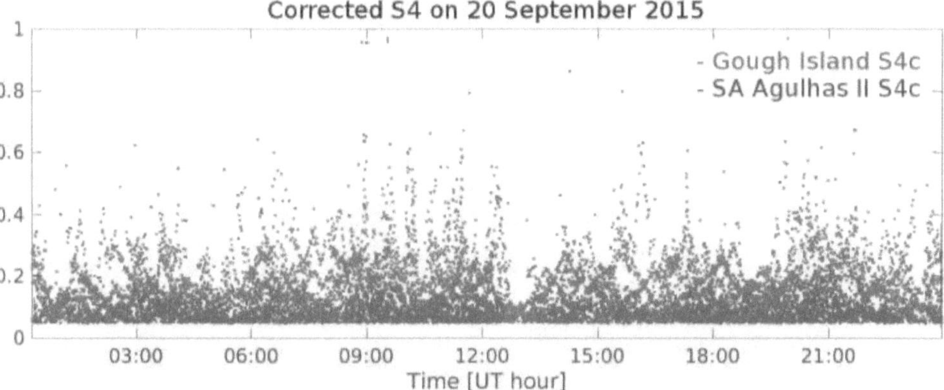

Figure 5.5: The corrected S_4 for 20 September 2015 from the ship and Gough Island are overlaid. The S_4 remains below 0.2 most of the time with occasional outliers. The SA Agulhas II values fluctuate up to three times higher, spiking multiple times throughout the day.

5.5 Identification of scintillation by other proxies

Other graphs from 20 September 2015 are shown in Figures 5.6 through 5.8. The presence of scintillation would be observed as ripples in the Vertical TEC; the VTEC for 20 September 2015 from Gough Island showed no sign of rapid variations in the electron density of the ionosphere.

The GPS satellite elevation and lock time results for Gough Island on 20 September 2015 were inspected but no extraordinary behaviour was observed. The SA Agulhas II, however, did experience a loss of lock in PRN 32 at 09:30 during the geomagnetic storm period (See Figure 5.7). The C/N_o graph for PRN32 on 20 September 2015 from the SA Agulhas II was presented in Figure 4.8 where a coinciding short-duration deep fade of almost 10 dB was observed at 09:30.

This concurrent behaviour is usually considered a good indicator of scintillation however the absence of a corresponding loss of lock or C/No fade in any the Gough Island data for the same period invalidates any such supposition. The effects of the geomagnetic storm on 20 September 2015 did not extend into the SAMA to Gough Island. However, the elevation of PRN32 when loss of lock occurred from the SA Agulhas II was roughly 20°; this may have been a contributing factor.

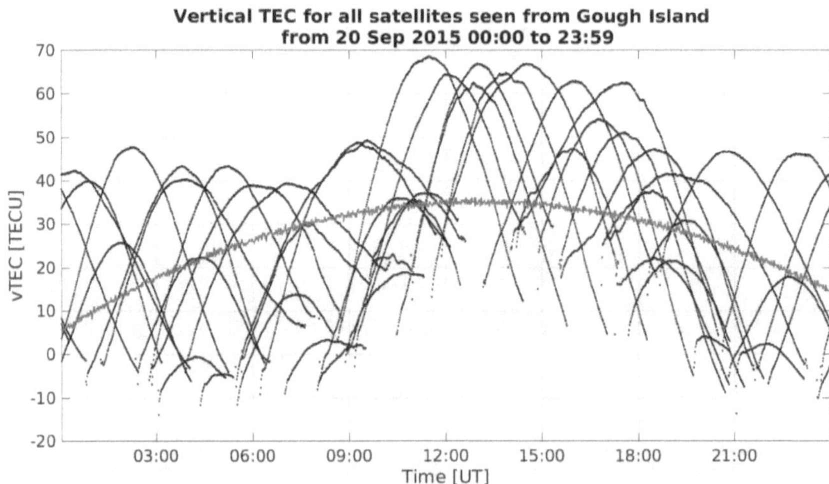

Figure 5.6: The Vertical TEC recorded from Gough Island on 20 September across all PRN is shown to be unaffected by the geomagnetic storm conditions. No ripples or disconnects are visible, making it unlikely that scintillation occurred.

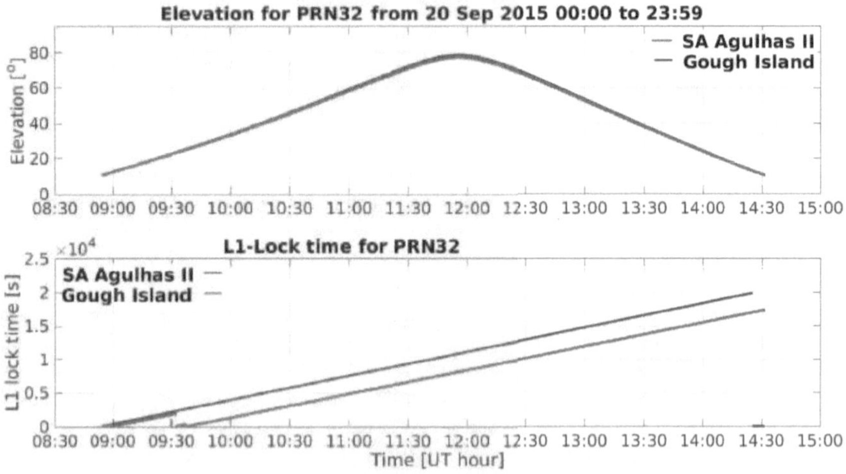

Figure 5.7: The elevation and lock time of PRN32 on 20 September shows loss of lock occurred at 09:30 in only the SA Agulhas II data. The Gough Island connection remained stable and the total lock time reached 20000 s before the satellite was no longer visible. The SA Agulhas II remained connected to PRN32 for ∼17500 s.

5.6 The effects of noise on position accuracy

A primary reason for studying scintillation is because of the effect it can have on GNSS accuracy. The motion of the ship, however, has been shown to introduce significant noise to the scintillation data. Real ionospheric scintillations can have a deleterious effect on the accuracy of the position estimates. In order to determine whether the motion-induced noise produced any position errors, the absolute position error distribution is calculated for both the SA Agulhas II and Gough Island GISTMs. The results for 20 September 2015 are shown in Figure 5.8.

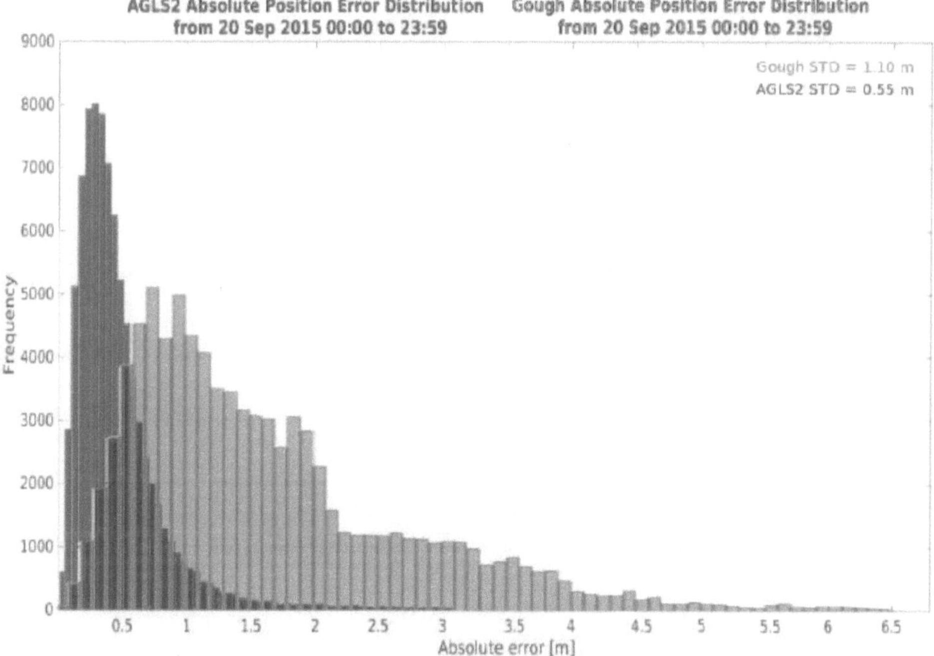

Figure 5.8: The absolute position error for 20 September 2015 for the SA Agulhas II and Gough Island were overlaid for comparison; the SA Agulhas II has a Stdev of half that of Gough Island (0.55 m v.s. 1.1 m) but a slightly higher peak frequency of 8000 counts over the 5000 of Gough Island.

The standard deviation (Stdev) of the SA Agulhas II antenna position for the day was 0.55 m while Gough Island's Stdev is twice as high, at 1.1 m. This result seems reversed as the stationary receiver is expected to be more accurate than the one in motion. The absolute position accuracy for 18 September 2015 is shown in Figure 5.9; again the SA Agulhas II has a lower Stdev (0.62 m) than Gough Island (0.85 m).

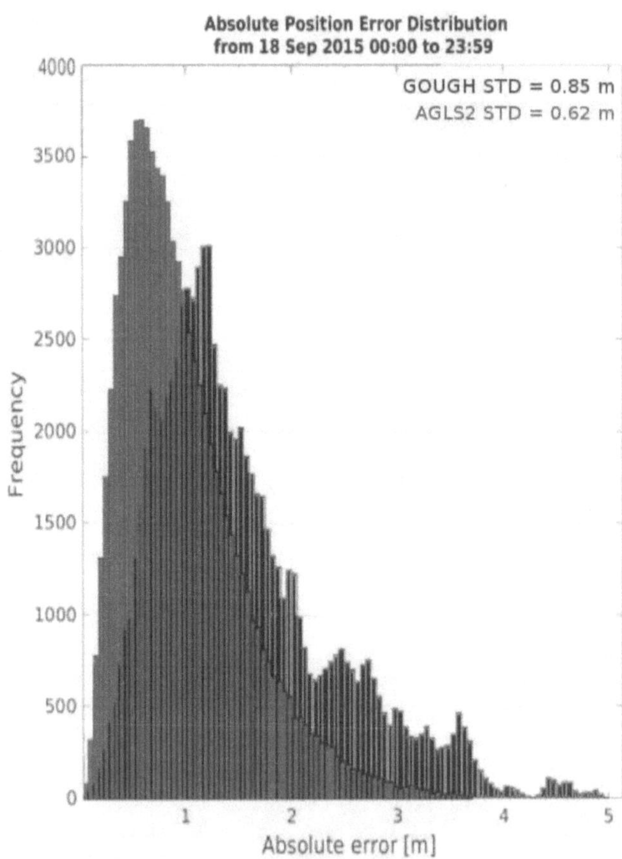

Figure 5.9: The absolute position error comparison for 18 September 2015 for the SA Agulhas II and Gough Island is presented. Once again the absolute position error values seem to be reversed but are in fact not; the island measures 0.85 m against the ship's 0.62 m. The Stdev of the ship is not always lower than that of the island, though, and an explanation is discussed in Section 5.6.

In contrast, on 26 September 2015 (graph not shown) the SA Agulhas II's absolute position Stdev was 5.36 m in comparison to the Gough Island absolute position Stdev of only 1.07 m; the peak frequency at the island was 5200 counts (1.0-1.1 m) while the ship's peak frequency was over 46000 counts (0-0.5 m). Further examination revealed that loss of lock was recorded across all satellites simultaneously at

16:30. This produced an instantaneous velocity of ∼1700 km/h which skewed the results.

The momentary gap in the recorded scintillation and TEC indices mimic the effect of a very strong scintillation which is why the various parameters cannot be studied in isolation. Ionospheric scintillation would only affect one, perhaps two satellites, but not all of them.

Further testing of the SA Agulhas II position errors were conducted using the X-Y position estimates, which is a horizontal error metric. This eliminates the ship's vertical displacement values from the calculation, leaving only the latitudinal and longitudinal components. The advantage of a scatter plot is that the size of the deviations can be visualised as well as the spatial distribution. Figure 5.10 shows the scatter plots for (a) the SA Agulhas II and (b) Gough Island. The SA Agulhas II had a Stdev of 0.53 m and the value for Gough Island was 0.5 m.

(a)   (b)

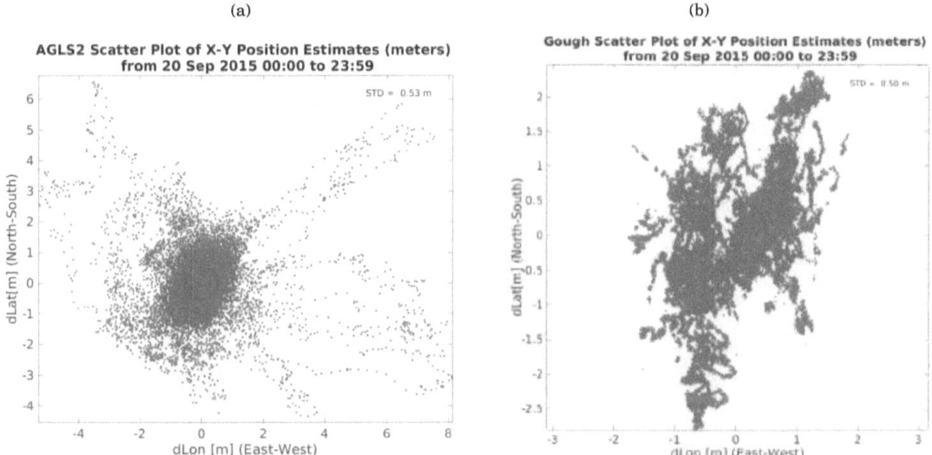

Figure 5.10: The X-Y position estimate shows the deviation, in meters, from the mean position of the antenna (0,0). (a): For the SA Agulhas II, the running mean was calculated over a 60-second window. The Stdev (indicated on the graph by the red circle) was 0.53 m. (b): The Gough Island X-Y position estimate made use of the true position of the antenna to calculate the deviations. The Stdev was 0.5 m which is comparable to the SA Agulhas II calculation.

The position error values for the island and the ship over the period 15-28 September were assessed. Barring exceptional circumstances such as those from 26 September 2015, the position errors of the SA Agulhas II were comparable to the position errors from Gough Island, even when the ship was moving at high speed. The conclusion was made that while the motion of the ship induced noise in the scintillation data, the position data remained unaffected and accurate.

This result is supported by practical evidence; even commercially available GPS systems such as those found inside a smartphone are capable of maintaining an accurate position estimate while travelling at high speeds such as in a vehicle or an aircraft.

5.7   The effect of satellite availability on position error.

The relationship between the number of GPS satellites tracked by the GISTM receiver and the horizontal error is demonstrated in Figure 5.11, recorded from the SA Agulhas II between 15-17 September 2015. Over the 3 day period, the number of satellites tracked by the GISTM receiver varied between 5-10. The most regular number of visible satellites is 9, followed by 8. No clear correlation is visible between the two parameters. Peaks in the horizontal error occurred during periods when 8-10 satellites were connected; Sometimes the error was low during when only 5-6 satellites were visible.

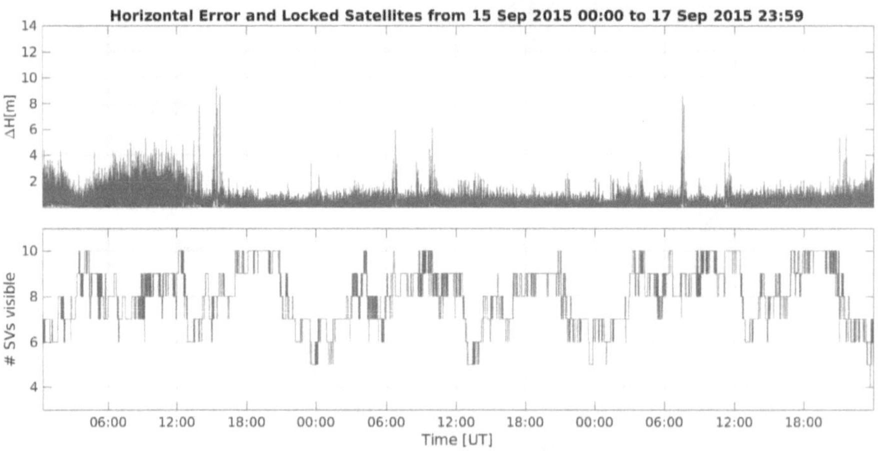

Figure 5.11: This graph shows the relationship between horizontal error and the number of available GPS satellites. No clear correlation was visible as the horizontal error was more affected by the velocity of the ship than the satellite count. When more than 6 satellites are available, the contribution to the position accuracy from each subsequent lock is smaller.

It was determined that the peaks in the horizontal error bore a closer resemblance to the change in velocity of the ship; sustained high-intensity movement of the antenna was correlated with sustained, moderate errors while the spikes in the velocity coincided with spikes in the horizontal error. This, however, is not a GPS-related issue but is rather simply a numeric reaction to the rapid change observed as the mathematical mean varies during the moving 60-second window. This is because the algorithm used to calculate the errors differs between the stationary and fixed use cases.

In addition, the contribution factor towards the position accuracy of a GPS unit declines with the addition of more satellites above a certain limit. 4 GPS satellites are required for a fundamental position fix in 3-dimensional space; adding a 5th provides an increase to the position accuracy. However, the contribution of the 6th satellite is far less, and the contribution from a 7th is very low. Any additional satellites provide a negligible increase in the position accuracy. If the number of available satellites were to decrease to 4, the effect on the horizontal position accuracy would be more significant.

The geometric distribution of the satellites can also have an effect on the accuracy of the position estimate. In any instance where the accuracy is degraded without an apparent cause the Dilution of Precision (DOP) should be checked. The DOP for 15 September 2015 from the location of the Gough Island GISTM is shown in Figure 2.13. The DOP for 17 September 2015 from the SA Agulhas II located 2 km offshore east of the base on Gough Island is shown in Figure 5.12. The DOP ratios were classified as very good, with a maximum of 3 . 1. The DOP was checked for unusual levels coinciding with all notable events observed in this research but it did not appear to be a contributing factor to position errors.

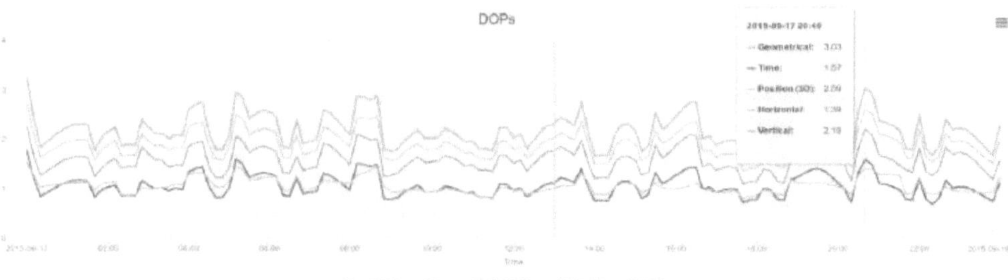

Figure 5.12: The calculated DOP values are shown for 17 September 2015 from a location 2 km east of the Gough Island base where the SA Agulhas II often held position. The graph was generated using Trimble (2018). The ideal DOP value is 1, however 2–3 is still considered very good. Values of 20 and higher are considered poor, and position errors on the order of hundreds of meters can be expected.

5.8   Recurring C/N_o fades and loss of lock in PRN32

Scintillations are rapid, short-duration events which can be identified by their 'extraordinary' effects on trans-ionospheric radio waves. Scintillation is not expected to recur predictably on a daily basis. A recurring dip and associated loss of lock was observed in the carrier-to-noise-density ratio of PRN 32 as recorded from the SA Agulhas II but not from Gough Island. Given the periodic nature of the C/No fade it is unlikely to have been caused by ionospheric scintillation.

THe C/No graph for PRN32 on 16 September 2015 was shown in Figure 4.8, and the C/No graphs for 19, 22, 23, and 24 September 2015 are shown in Figures 5.13 through 5.16. The recurring fade of up to 10 dB is clearly visible every day at around 09:30. The Gough Island C/N_o remained unaffected.

The C/N_o fades began near the start of the satellite transits. The lock time and elevation maps for 22 and 24 September are shown in Figures 5.17 and 5.18. Recurring loss of lock congruent with the C/N_o fades were identified. An analysis of the transit geometry of PRN32 indicated that it rose at azimuth 230° (south-west) and had a peak elevation of 80°.

Position data for the SA Agulhas II revealed that each day, at 09:30, the ship was located on the south-eastern coast of the island near the Gough Island base. The difficulty experienced in maintaining a lock on PRN32 may have been caused by interference in the line of sight at that azimuth, however this cannot be confirmed without additional information. On 24 September 2015 (Figure 5.18), the loss of lock persisted until PRN32 reached an elevation of 40°, which is high enough that not even the mountain peaks of Gough Island could block the line of sight.

The velocity data of the SA Agulhas II confirmed that it was stationary during each of the fades. It is thus unlikely that the motion of the ship was responsible. Further research would be required to determine the cause of these recurring fades.

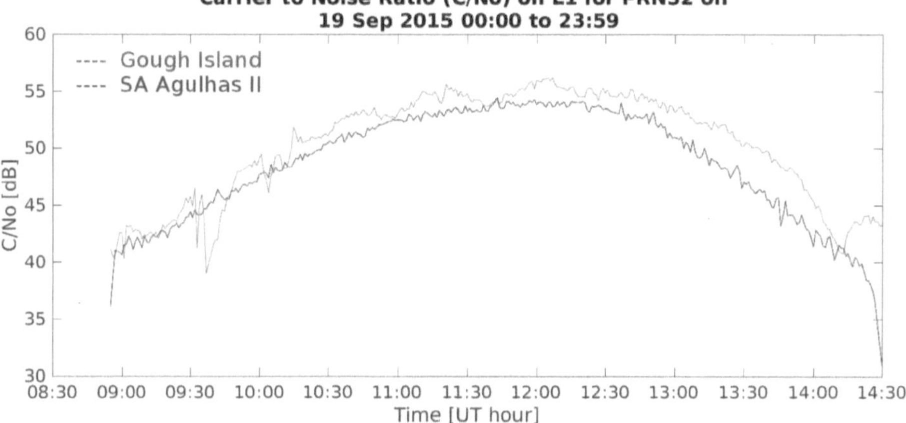

Figure 5.13: This graph shows the L1 C/N_o for PRN32 on 19 September 2015 for both the SA Agulhas II and Gough Island. A fade of ~8 dB begin at 09:30, dropping to a C/N_o of 38 dB in roughly 15 minutes. By 09:45 the C/N_o recorded from the SA Agulhas II had recovered from the fade. The Gough Island C/N_o seen in this graph is a very typical curve ranging between 40-55 dB.

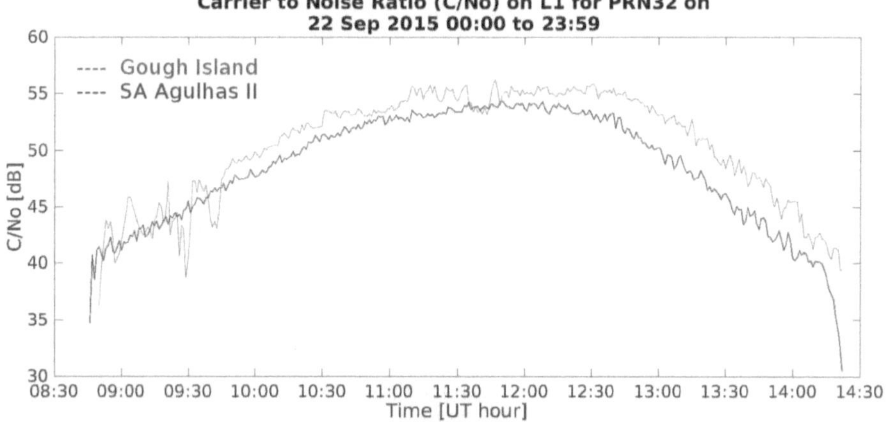

Figure 5.14: The L1 C/N_o for PRN32 on 22 September 2015 for both the SA Agulhas II and Gough Island are shown. The C/N_o recorded from the ship shows variations of ~5 dB preceding a larger fade of nearly 10 dB at 09:30. Another 5 dB fluctuation was seen at 09:45 before the C/N_o curve normalised.

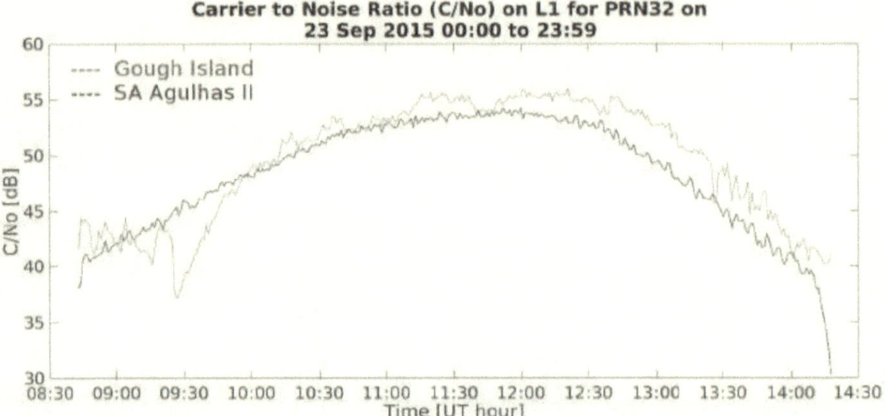

Figure 5.15: This graph shows the L1 C/N_o for PRN32 on 23 September 2015 from the SA Agulhas II overlaid with the corresponding Gough Island C/N_o data. A series of small fluctuations of <5 dB precede the deep fade which reaches it minimum of 37 dB at 09:30, before recovering up to 10 dB to normal values over a half-hour. The Gough Island C/N_o curve remains stable during the entire transit of PRN32.

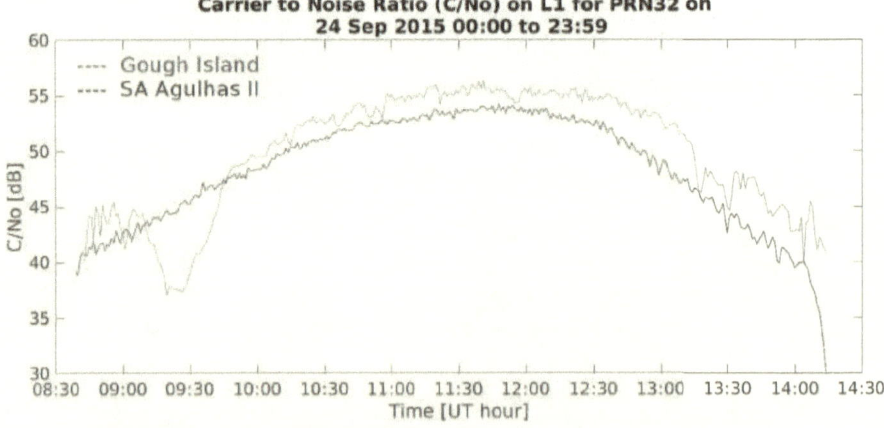

Figure 5.16: This graph shows the L1 C/N_o for PRN32 on 24 September 2015 for both the SA Agulhas II and Gough Island. The SA Agulhas II data features an almost 10 dB deep, and 45-minute wide, fade in the signal. A few smaller fluctuations precede the main event, which reaches a minimum of 37 dB shortly before 09:30 and maintains that value for nearly 10 minutes.

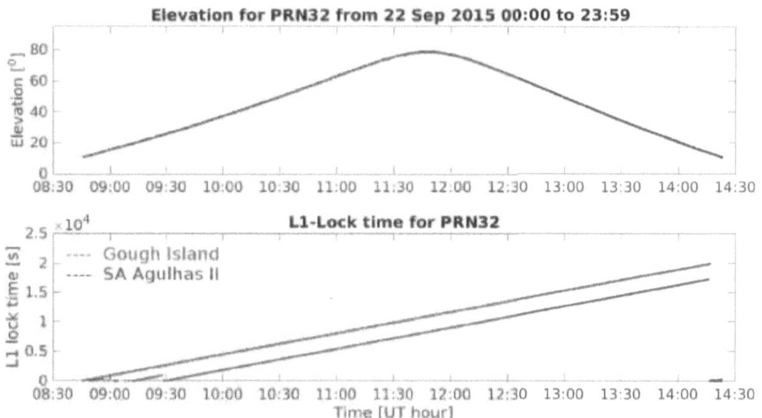

Figure 5.17: The loss of lock from the SA Agulhas II receiver to PRN 32 is clearly visible in this graph for 22 September 2015. The Gough Island data indicates a normal signal acquisition and satellite transit. The SA Agulhas II struggled to secure an initial lock, and the one established at 09:15 was lost again at 09:30. The signal was reacquired quickly and the remainder of PRN32's transit was uneventful, with the satellite reaching a peak elevation of 80°.

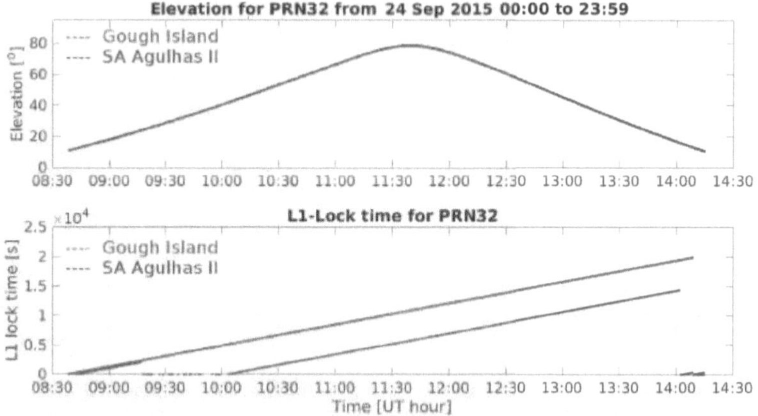

Figure 5.18: This graph shows the Lock time and Elevation for PRN32 on 24 September 2015 for both the SA Agulhas II and Gough Island. Both GISTMs obtain a lock initially. At 09:20, the deep, wide C/N_o fade observed in Figure 5.16 caused loss of lock from the SA Agulhas II, and then suppressed the signal re-acquisition repeatedly for 40 minutes. The satellite had already reached an elevation above 40° before the signal locked on again for the rest of the transit.

5.9   Identification of additional noise sources

On the morning of 18 September 2015 the SA Agulhas II GISTM recorded multiple, persistent loss of lock events across several GPS satellites, including PRN8 and PRN27. Fades of up to 10 dB were seen in the C/N_o at the same time. This is usually a good proxy for scintillation, however, neither the loss of lock nor the C/N_o fades were found in the Gough Island data. Scintillation due to ionospheric electron density fluctuations would most likely have occurred in both sets of data.

Figure 5.19 shows the C/N_o for PRN27 overlaid on the elevation and lock time curves for 18 September 2015. Figure 5.20 is a composite of the corrected S_4, σ_ϕ and C/N_o on PRN8 for the same day. The elevation of the GPS satellites were fairly low, with PRN8 rising to 20° (07:05-09:20) and PRN27 reaching a maximum elevation of 30° (05:35-09:00). The repeated loss of lock occurred throughout these same periods. Both PRN8 and PRN27 were visible again in the afternoon with elevations above 40° and 60° respectively, with no loss of lock.

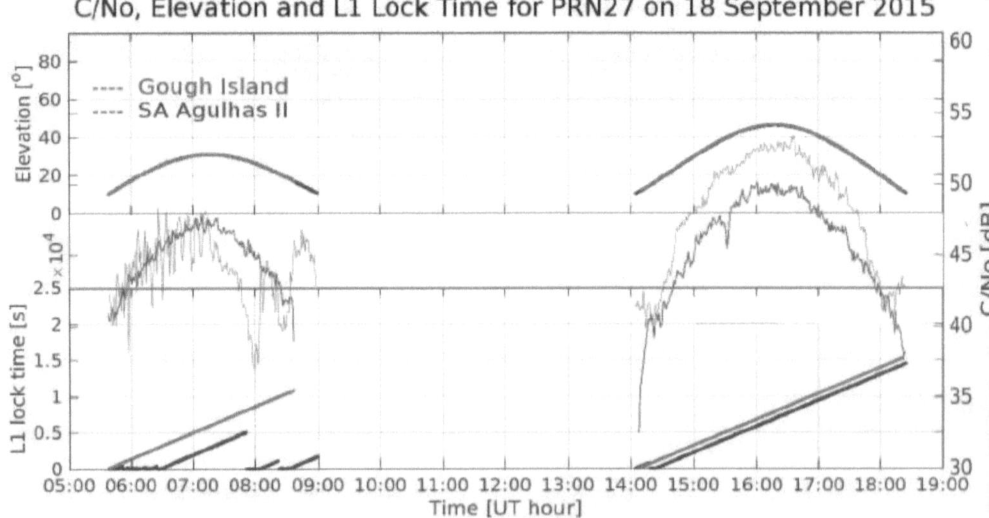

Figure 5.19: A composite image of the C/N_o, elevation and lock time for PRN27 from 18 September 2015 is shown here. The morning C/N_o from the SA Agulhas II showed rapid fluctuations of up to 5 dB, followed by a deep fade of 10 dB. The GPS receiver lock on PRN27 struggled to stabilise until the satellites reached a 30° elevation. The deep fade coincided with the loss of lock at 07:45, when PRN27 had returned to 30°. Loss of lock takes place at least twice more during this transit.

Both PRN8 and PRN27 were only visible in the south-west quadrant during the low-elevation transit. While the low elevation angle does naturally increase the risk of signal absorption, multipath errors, and

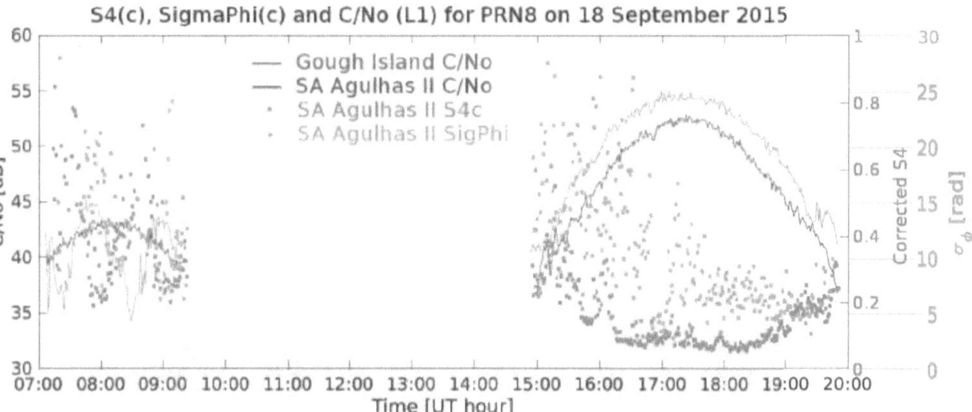

Figure 5.20: The S_4, σ_ϕ and C/N_o recorded from PRN8 on 18 September 2015 are combined in this graph. Only two major fades are visible in the SA Agulhas II's C/N_o during the morning transit of PRN8; the second dropped by 11 dB down to a minimum of 34 dB at 08:30. The corrected S_4 values appears to be inversely proportional to the C/N_o values. When the C/N_o increases, the S_4 decreases. The distribution of the σ_ϕ narrows unusually during the second transit. Before 17:00 the σ_ϕ showed the expected distribution (up to 30 rad), however after 17:00 the distribution narrows to below 10 rad. Figure 5.21 describes this anomaly in greater detail.

encountering electron density variations which cause scintillation, the loss of lock of the signals took place over a range of elevations, not just at the rising and setting of the satellites.

The possibility of low-level obstructions could not be dismissed, either. Given the evidence of motion-induced noise discovered in this research, the velocity and σ_ϕ values were also investigated (see Figure 5.21) but showed no particular correlation to the loss of lock. The $S4$ also remained at nominal levels throughout the day.

It was noted, however, that the σ_ϕ-velocity relationship exhibited an unusual pattern after 17:00. The SA Agulhas II maintained a constant, low-level speed between 2.5-5 km/h throughout the day until the 10 km/h peak visible at 17:00, and then returned to constant, low-level activity. The σ_ϕ exhibited the expected wide distribution (up to 30 rad) due to the motion-induced noise until the ship's change in position at 17:00. After 17:00 the σ_ϕ distribution inexplicably narrowed to <10 rad despite the maintained velocity.

Position information revealed that the SA Agulhas II was located off the south-western coast of Gough Island until 17:00, at which point it relocated to a position east of the island near the research base. The location of the ship during the morning transits of PRN8 and PRN27 rule out the possibility of obstructions

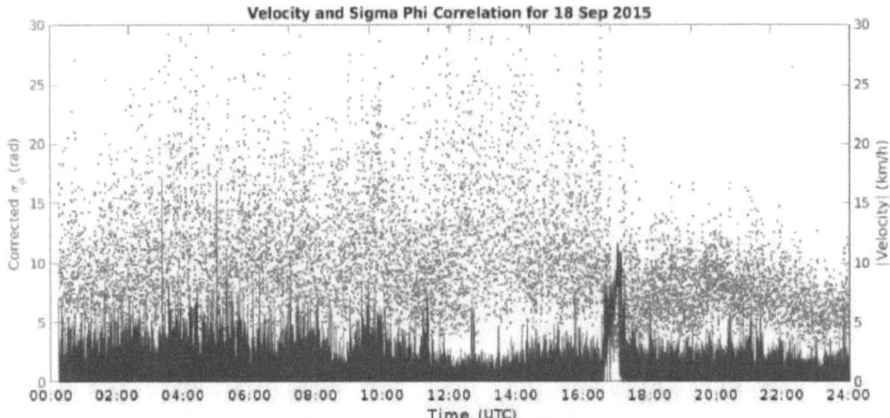

Figure 5.21: The correlation between the velocity of the SA Agulhas II GISTM and the corrected σ_ϕ for 18 September 2015 is shown in this plot. The σ_ϕ values are distributed widely (up to 30 rad) as has been shown to be the norm for motion-affected scintillation data, especially considering the presence of a persistent low-velocity reading. This normal response changes after 17:00 when the SA Agulhas II relocated to the eastern side of the island to take shelter from high winds. The σ_ϕ distribution then narrowed to below 10 rad despite the ship continuing to function at a persistent low-velocity. The hypothesis derived from this observation is that the wind could be a contributing factor to the motion noise effect.

as a clear line of sight was available. 18 September 2015 was also a geomagnetically quiet day as seen in Figure 5.3.

According to researchers who were on board the SA Agulhas II at the time in question, the relocation was prompted by unfavourable wind conditions. Flight operations were imminent, but the persistent, high wind speeds presented a safety risk. The ship sailed around the island in search of wind-shelter for the helicopters. The change in position, and the drop in wind speed are the only two movement-related factors identified which could have affected the σ_ϕ to that extent.

This generated a new hypothesis that the wind may be a contributing factor to the enhanced scintillation values recorded by the SA Agulhas II GISTM. Future research may take into account this new variable.

In this project, the amplitude scintillation (S_4) and phase scintillation (σ_ϕ) indices from 50 Hz L1 GPS signals recorded during the 2014 and 2015 voyages of the SA Agulhas II were analysed for the first time. The goal of the research was to assess the challenges of using a moving GISTM receiver to obtain accurate scintillation data and to also attempt to identify instances of ionospheric scintillation within the unique magnetic environment of the South Atlantic Magnetic Anomaly using the recorded data.

The mechanisms which cause scintillation in equatorial regions are well known, but scintillation due to auroral patches is not yet as well understood. For mid-latitudes it is only known that scintillations are rare. They are most likely to only be seen during a strong geomagnetic storm as high levels of particle precipitation accompanied by an expanded auroral oval reaching the mid-latitudes are required to induce scintillation.

Since this research looks for the first time at ionospheric scintillation data recorded from a moving platform within the SAMA there were very few known behaviours that could be expected from the data in advance of the analysis. Extensive reviews of relevant literature provided information such as general thresholds and known variations between equatorial and high-latitude studies; the observations from mid-latitude studies in regions outside of the SAMA were also taken into consideration.

6.1 Objectives achieved

Nearly all of the stated objectives (see Section 1.2) of this research were achieved. A cross-referenced summary of the outcomes of each objective is shown below. The number in brackets after each case indicates the relevant section of this book where the particular aspect of the work was presented.

1. The cause, full extent of, and solutions to the configuration problems of the NovAtel GSV4004B GISTM on the SA Agulhas II were determined. Corrections were implemented to the GPS epoch,

leap seconds, and system time discrepancies. (3.5)

2. Updates were performed on the software necessary to convert the GISTM data to accessible formats and perform initial tests. Additional scripts were developed to correct the misalignment in the data sets which resulted from the system time discrepancies. Data management was implemented to structure the data into appropriate sets. (A.1)

3. The presence of noise in the SA Agulhas II scintillation data was established by the wide range of values recorded in comparison to the normal accepted global ranges. The primary source of the noise was identified as the motion of the SA Agulhas II through comparisons with data from an identical stationary receiver located near the ship. The general effect of the motion on the magnitude of the noisy data was shown through analysis in relation to the author's personally experienced movements of the SA Agulhas II. (4.1, 4.4).

4. The orientation of the antenna on the SA Agulhas II relative to the horizon was examined to determined the tolerance of the system against multipath errors. This was done to determine if any additional factors were contributing to noise in the recorded data. (3.3)

5. A frequency response analysis was performed on the movement of the SA Agulhas II in search of the dominant frequencies. The 1-second time resolution of the movement data was found to be too low to identify the frequencies needed for the development of a filter. It was thus not possible to filter the motion-induced noise out of the data being used for this research. The use of position data with a higher sampling rate to derive a front-end filter for high sampling rate amplitude and phase data could prove more successful. (4.7)

6. MATLAB was used to develop a set of customised programs for the detailed analysis of the scintillation and position data from a moving receiver. This included the development of a running mean algorithm for determining position errors in moving receivers. A second set of MATLAB programs was developed for use in the analysis of stationary receiver data. (A.2)

7. Scintillation could not be identified from the SA Agulhas II data as the motion-induced noise masked any potential scintillation events across all the parameters used as proxies. Additionally, the 1-minute time resolution of the scintillation data may be too low to identify short-duration scintillation events. This objective, which was central to the purpose of this entire research project, could not be achieved. (5.2)

8. The noisy data from the SA Agulhas II was compared against data from the stationary receiver on Gough Island for a period when the two GISTMs were within 100 km of each other. The results obtained indicated that, despite the inability to identify ionospheric scintillation, the results obtained from the other parameters were comparable to those from Gough Island. (4.3, 5.5)

Scintillation was not detected in the Gough Island data despite the indicated presence of a moderate geomagnetic storm. A brief comparison was done with a third GISTM location outside the SAMA:

the GISTM installed at the SANAE-IV research base in Antarctica. The Gough Island data was assumed to be accurate as the auroral oval probably did not extend far enough towards the equator to produce precipitation-induced mid-latitude scintillations. (5.3, 5.4)

9. The data from the SA Agulhas II GISTM still contained useful information about the correlations between the various recorded parameters. The relationships between these parameters were explored as well as the effect of the motion-induced noise on these parameters. It was found that the overall accuracy of the determination of the position of the SA Agulhas II was not affected by the motion-induced noise, and that the use of a running mean algorithm for moving receivers produces results which are comparable to those of a stationary receiver. (4.6, 5.5, 5.6, 5.8)

The SA Agulhas II horizontal position error was also not observed as being affected by the number of connected GPS satellites, a metric which is affected by scintillation through loss of lock. Lastly, unusual behaviour in the velocity-σ_ϕ relationship presented evidence that additional external factors may be contributing to the motion-noise effect. (5.7, 5.9)

6.2 Unique findings

Several unique observations were made. A summary of these discoveries is as follows:

- The NovAtel GSV4004B GISTM has a hard-coded threshold in the onboard software; in this instance all data from satellites with an elevation angle below $10°$ was automatically excluded from the recordings. This is generally accepted practice in scintillation studies as receivers are usually located in areas with some form of low-level obstructions. In the unique case of the SA Agulhas II, there are no obstructions on the open ocean, and the data from elevation angles in the of $0°$-$10°$ may have been of scientific interest. (3.3)

- The SA Agulhas II was calculated to have a roll angle threshold of $20°$ before the GISTM's automatic $10°$ elevation cut-off would be reached and multipath signals from the horizon would be entering the GISTM antenna at an elevation angle above the $10°$ internal mask. The ship does not roll more than $10°$ from vertical during normal operations and therefore no multipath was likely to be experienced. (3.3)

- It was discovered and confirmed that the SA Agulhas II's motion introduces significant noise into the scintillation data as indicated by the S_4 and σ_ϕ parameters. (4.4, 4.7)

- The motion-induced noise manifested primarily in the σ_ϕ (phase scintillation) data. The S_4 (amplitude scintillation) was only mildly affected, and in a more consistent manner. The SA Agulhas II S_4 readings were on the same order of magnitude, with a consistent distribution measuring up to 3 times the value of the Gough Island S_4, and varying in the same patterns. In contrast, the SA Agulhas II σ_ϕ values were up to 300 times those of the Gough Island σ_ϕ, with variations in the distribution which did not correspond to the Gough Island σ_ϕ patterns. (4.1, 4.4, 4.5.6, 4.5.9, 4.7)

- The σ_ϕ noise distribution and magnitude were confirmed to be proportional to the velocity of the SA Agulhas II. The duration of the motion of the SA Agulhas II also impacted the width of the σ_ϕ distribution; sustained periods of low velocity movement produced more noise than short-duration high-speed displacements. (5.2)

- No scintillation events were identified using the SA Agulhas II GISTM between 15-28 September 2015, however, the Gough Island GISTM data also showed no significant scintillation events during the same period, despite the confirmed presence of a moderate geomagnetic storm on 20 September 2015. Data from the SANAE-IV GISTM confirmed that scintillation did result from this storm at high latitudes. (5.2, 5.3, 5.4, 5.5)

- Relationships were discovered between (a) velocity and σ_ϕ, (b) the rate of change of velocity with the horizontal error, (c) C/N_o and S_4, and (d) C/N_o and lock time. (5.2, 5.5, 5.6, 5.8, 5.7, 5.9)

- It was noted that motion-induced noise in the SA Agulhas II scintillation data had no effect on the position accuracy of the moving receiver. (4.6, 5.6)

- Although it is known that the more GPS satellites there are visible to the receiver, the better the position estimate will be, the SA Agulhas II data did not show a recognisable correlation between the horizontal position error and the number of GPS satellites which was attributed to the high availability of GPS satellites in the SAMA region where the SA Agulhas II and Gough Island were located. (5.6)

- An unusual variation in the behaviour of the velocity-σ_ϕ relationship on 18 September 2015 was identified. The distribution of the SA Agulhas II's σ_ϕ values was reduced to one-third despite velocity being maintained. The ship had relocated around the island in search of shelter from high winds, and it was theorised that wind may be a contributing factor to the motion noise. (5.9)

6.3   Research Outcomes

SANSA Space Science accepted the proof that the movement of the SA Agulhas II introduced significant levels of noise to the data recorded by the NovAtel GSV4004B GISTM, preventing it from detecting scintillation events as was its intended purpose. This provided the justification needed for the financing and procurement of a new, motion-compensated GAMMA receiver from ASTRA.

The new asset was installed on the SA Agulhas II in July 2017 and has since then been operating in parallel with the GISTM on a shared antenna. The improved scintillation data will hopefully allow researchers to identify large-scale scintillation structures in the ionosphere, improving our understanding of particle precipitation linked to the unusual magnetic conditions within the SAMA.

6.4 Future work

Several potential research projects were identified through this work.

The high-time-resolution NVD files also recorded by the SA Agulhas II GISTM could be used in the development of a filter for the motion-induced noise. The amplitude and phase data from the NVD files should also be examined for evidence of scintillation-related changes during strong geomagnetic storms which occurred during periods when the SA Agulhas II was sailing to any destination. This may provide greater insight as to the scientific value of the ionospheric scintillation data recorded to date while the SA Agulhas II was in motion.

A comparison study between the 'old' GISTM and the 'new' GAMMA receivers on the SA Agulhas II could be performed to quantify the improvement made by the motion-compensation algorithms of the GAMMA, and also to fulfil the original objective of this research: to identify scintillation inside the SAMA using a mobile terrestrial receiver.

Lastly, additional research could be undertaken to determine what role, if any, the wind may have in the noise produced by the motion of the antenna of the GISTM on the SA Agulhas II.

A.1   Scripting

Appendix A contains detailed descriptions of the various scripts used to process the GISTM data. The languages used were Bash, Python, Ruby, and MATLAB.

A.1.1   PSN Concatenation Script

A Bash script was written for concatenation of hourly PSN files to daily files for ease of use. The script was run for each year individually (2014, 2015, 2016). The concatenated PSN files were then copied out to a separate working location as a year's worth of full, raw data from the GISTMs amounts to approximately 180 GB. The *.nvd data composes the bulk of the file size; a day's worth is on the order of 500 MB. In comparison, a day of ISM data averages 2.5 MB and a day of PSN data is roughly 6.7 MB.

```
#!/bin/bash          # PSNcopycat.sh #

#This script was used to CAT and copy only the DAILY PSN files out of the FULL DATA SET
#Only the PSN files were needed for Positioning assessment
#The FULL DATA set is so large that it cannot be worked with all the time
#This was a once-off action #Created by Ani Vermeulen and JG Vermeulen (2016)

targetyr=2014 #Choose the year to work with, repeat manually for other years
sourceyr="FullData"$targetyr        #'FullData2014' - source file name
targetfile="PSNFull"$targetyr       #'PSNFull2014' - destination file for daily PSN

for year in $targetyr ; do {
for month in `ls $sourceyr` ; do {
        mkdir -p $targetfile/$month
        for day in `ls $sourceyr/$month`  ; do {
            wd=$year/$month/$day/
            date=$targetyr'-'$month'-'$day
```

```
            echo "Day signifier is: "$date
                cd $wd
                cat psn/*.psn > $date"Dailypsn.psn"
                echo "Daily PSN file created: "$date"Dailypsn.psn"
            #Return to root of GST directory
            cd ../../../
            cp $sourceyr/$month/$day/*.psn $targetfile/$month/
            echo $month"/"$day"/psn DAILY FILE created and copied."
            echo " "
        }; done            #End days loop
    }; done            #End month loop
}; done            #End year
```

A.1.2   ISM Concatenation & Plotting Script

Another Bash script was written to manage the hourly ISM files. Firstly, the ISM files needed to be concatenated into a temporary daily ISM file. This was then parsed into plain text format by calling the parseismr script developed by NovAtel for the GSV4004B system. It is important to note that parseismr has an accompanying configuration file, defaults.cfg, which is used to specify a few options provided by the parsing script, such as an elevation cut-off. The temporary daily ISM binary file was then deleted.

The σ_ϕ and S_4 values in the ISM text file were then plotted by calling a python script, AGLS_Bins_2016_v1.py as an immediate test of the proper conversion of the ISM data. This daily histogram script is discussed in Appendix A.1.3.

```
#!/bin/bash ISMcopycat.sh

#This script is used to concatenate, parse, and generate image files from the ISM files.
#This script runs per year, and needs to be repeated for each year, manually amended.
#This script copies several files into destination folders and then runs them.
#This script calls/copies:
#        - AGLS_Bins_2016_v1.py   - This is the Scintillation daily histogram script
#        - defaults.cfg           - This is the configuration file for parseismr
#        - parseismr              - This is the parsing program, converts ISM binary to TXT
#OUTPUT:
#        - Converted.txt          - A daily text file version of the ISM data
#        - AGLS-GST1_(date).pdf   - a daily PDF graph showing the SigmaPhi and S4 values
#Developed by Ani Vermeulen, with assistance from JG Vermeulen, July 2016
#The files used by this script were not developed by this script's author.
#The concept for this script is based on the script combine_plot.sh by Jon Ward, SANSA


years="2015"              #Choose year to loop
# Loop over all subdirectories in year
for year in $years ; do {
    for month in `ls $year` ; do {
        for day in `ls $year/$month`; do {

            wd=$year/$month/$day
```

```
#Copy Python script and config file, and change working directory
#echo ">> Step1: Copying AGLS Python script and defaults.cfg to " $wd
cp AGLS_Bins_2016_v1.py defaults.cfg parseismr ./$wd
#echo ">> Step2: Change working directory to " $wd
cd $wd

#Combine 24 1-hr files into a single daily temporary combination ISM file
cat ism/*.ism > temp.ism
#echo ">> Step3: Concatenation achieved. Temp file created."

#Parse the daily ISM into a txt file using parseismr (1-1024, all, or azel)
#chmod gives parseismr permission to run as an executable (NB!)
chmod ug+x parseismr
./parseismr all temp.ism Converted.txt
#echo ">> Step4: Parsing of ism data to text format complete."

#Now generate the image (runs AGLS-Bins Py script in same file)
python AGLS_Bins_2016_v1.py
#echo ">> Step5: Image generation script run."

#Remove temporary combination ISM file
rm temp.ism
#echo ">> Step6: Temp file removed."
#echo " "
#echo " "

#Return to root of GST directory
cd ../../../


        #echo
    }; done      #End day loop
  }; done         #End month loop
}; done           #End year loop
```

A.1.3 Daily Histogram Script

The `AGLS_Bins_2016_v1.py` daily histogram script was based on SANSA's Marion Island daily histogram script (by Jonathan Ward). It is intended as both an initial test of the fidelity of the parsed ISM data, and to quickly test whether the GSV4004B System was functioning properly. By running the script daily over an entire year, it provided a fast way to compare successive days and identify any anomalies or interesting results.

The daily histogram script applies several filters and processing on the ISM data. This includes only selecting the GPS PRNs (1-32), an elevation cut-off option (again), testing for the correct value of $S_4 c$, and removing outliers ($\sigma_\phi > 10$, $S_4 > 2$). It counts the number of scintillation events which exceed a selected limit (number of $\sigma_\phi > 0.2$, number of $S_4 > 0.2$), and plots this as a histogram. For Ubuntu users, the Python `numpy` and `matplotlib` packages are required.

This script is capable of handling either raw ISM files or converted text files. Since the `parseismr` program was already run to parse the scintillation data to plain text format, this built-in conversion feature was not used.

The script is also responsible for the conversion of GPS time (GPS Week and Time of Week) to regular time (`YYYY MM DD HH:MM:SS`) for use in plotting. The full script is over 400 lines of Python code, so it is not replicated here. The SA Agulhas II script can be made available on request from the author, or the original version may be requested from SANSA.

The daily histograms provided the first indication of problems with the data set. Every graph generated for the SA Agulhas II consistently showed missing data at the end of the data files. The data files themselves were investigated and it was determined that the first entry for each day was at 22:08 the night before. An example of an affected daily histogram is shown in Figure A.1.

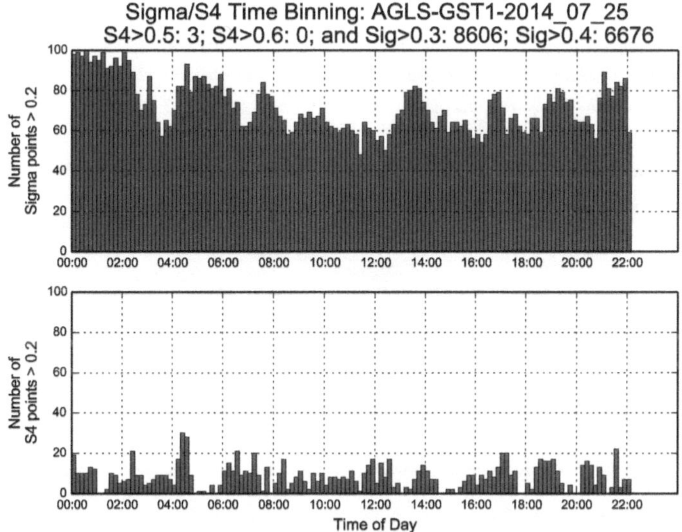

Figure A.1: An example of a daily histogram generated by `AGLS_Bins_2016_v1.py` for 25 July 2014. The missing data towards the end of the day can clearly be seen. This occurred on all the initial SA Agulhas II daily histograms.

A.1.4   Ruby Data File Correction Script

This Ruby script, `ani_v2.rb`, was created in collaboration with coder extraordinaire Toby Kurien from House4Hack. Sincere thanks go to him for his willing assistance and diligence.

The handling of 'next day' and 'previous day' directives in programming can be complicated, and Python was not conducive to achieving the data management objective. Ruby has built-in commands to look up dates using a calendar. In this case, the command '`date.prev_day`' was simple and fast to implement.

The purpose is to copy the first two hourly files from the following day's folder to the day in question. The daily histogram script used the actual time stamps in the data file to compile the graph, not the file headings. It could then access and plot the previously missing 22:00-00:00 data, while ignoring the extraneous data from the day before.

The fix was first tested against automatically generated files, then against a dummy data set, and lastly against a copy of the actual data set. When all three tests passed successfully, the script was officially applied to the ISM and PSN files for the entire data set. A backup of the original data was retained anyway, just in case.

The conversion for use with the PSN files merely required changing the data directory, and amending the file extensions being searched for from `*.ism` to `*.psn`.

```ruby
#ani_v2.rb  -- A script for fixing the misaligned data file issue (used for both PSN and ISM)

require 'date'
require 'fileutils'

# Move first 2 hr ISM files from one day to the day before (2016)
# Developed by Toby Kurien, 16-Oct-2016, with Ani Vermeulen

DATA_DIR = "GST_Actual_Test" # full or relative path to ISM folder, e.g. /home/ani/Desktop/GST/ISMFiles/

months = %w{ 01-Jan 02-Feb 03-Mar 04-Apr 05-May 06-Jun
             07-Jul 08-Aug 09-Sep 10-Oct 11-Nov 12-Dec }

# Process existing directories as year/month/day
Dir.glob("#{DATA_DIR}/*").sort.select do |y|
    Dir.glob("#{y}/*").sort.select do |m|
        Dir.glob("#{m}/*").sort.select do |d|
            print "#{d}\n" # show what directory we are busy processing

            # extract the date from the directory structure so we can subtract a calendar day
            pathSplit = d.split("/")
            year = pathSplit[1].to_i
```

```
            month = pathSplit[2][0..1].to_i
            day = pathSplit[3].to_i
            begin
                date = Date.new(year, month, day) # this might fail if date invalid, e.g. Feb 30th
                tdate = date.prev_day # calculate previous day as per calendar

                # process all the ISM files
                Dir.glob("#{d}/ism/*").sort.select do |ism|
                    # work out target directory for moving files.
                    # Syntax note, this pads value of x with 0 if single digit: "%0.2d" % x
                    target = "#{pathSplit[0]}/#{tdate.year}/#{months[tdate.month - 1]}/#{"%0.2d" % tdate.day}/ism/"
                    begin
                      # look for ISM files with "_00" or "_01" anywhere in the file name
                      ["_00", "_01"].each do |key|
                        file= "#{d}/ism/#{date.year -2000}#{"%0.2d" % date.month}#{"%0.2d" % date.day}#{key}0000.ism"
                          if File.exist?(file)
                          # we found such a file, let's create target directory and move the file into it
                            print "- Moving #{file} to #{target}\n"
                            FileUtils.mkdir_p target if !File.exist?(target)
                            FileUtils.mv file, target
                          end
                        end
                    rescue => e
                        print "- ** ERROR ** #{e.message}\n"
                    end
                end if File.directory?(d)
            rescue => dateError
                print "- ** ERROR ** #{dateError.message} #{year}/#{month}/#{day}\n"
            end
        end if File.directory?(m)
    end if File.directory?(y)
end
```

This correction was the last one applied to the data before the scientific analysis could begin.
A copy of the 'clean' data was provided to SANSA for inclusion in their data warehouse, where it
can be accessed and used by other scientists. Thanks goes to data manager Kate Niemantinga for
her assistance with my numerous data queries and the uploads to the SANSA data portal.

After the data correction process was completed, the daily histograms discussed in Section
A.1.3 were generated again. The corrected version of Figure A.1 is shown in Figure A.2.

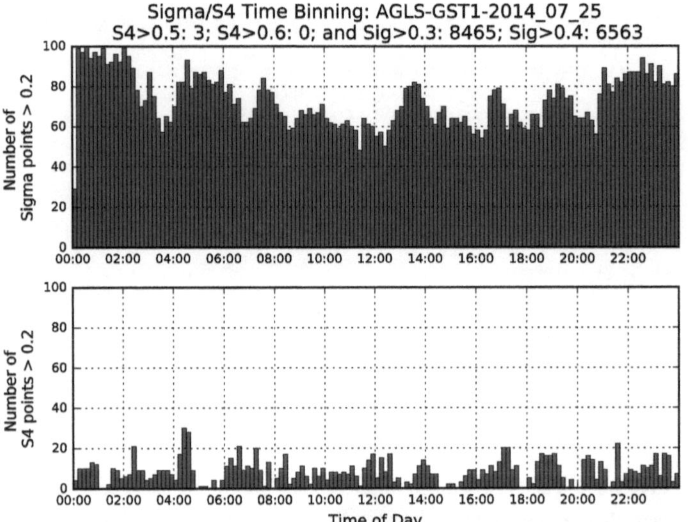

Figure A.2: An example of a corrected daily histogram, produced using `AGLS_Bins_2016_v1.py` for 25 July 2014, after the ISM data correction process was completed.

A.2 MATLAB Code Overview

The MATLAB code written for this research consisted of two main scripts, one for the scintillation (*.ism) analysis and one for the position (*.psn) calculations. Two versions of each were created in order to customise the scripts for both the stationary (Gough) and moving (SA Agulhas II) states. A total of four independent analysis scripts were thus used to complement the four main sets of data:

- ISM-AGLS2 - the moving *.ism scintillation data from the SA Agulhas II
- PSN-AGLS2 - the moving *.psn position data from the SA Agulhas II
- ISM-GOUGH - the stationary *.ism scintillation data from Gough Island
- PSN-GOUGH - the stationary *.psn position data from Gough Island

The full MATLAB code is not replicated in these appendices owing to their exceptionally large size. Each ISM script is over 1100 lines, and the PSN scripts are almost 750 lines long. Instead, a brief overview of the structure and objective of the scripts are provided in this section. The full MATLAB scripts can be made available upon request from the author or from SANSA.

A.2.1 MATLAB: ISM scripts

The fundamental scientific coding of the ISM script was based on previously developed scintillation processing functions written in MATLAB (Microsoft Windows version) by Dr Pierre Cilliers. These sections of code, and the formulas used, have been verified for use in properly calculating and processing the various scintillation indices recorded by the SANSA GISTMs.

The existing MATLAB code had to be reconfigured for Linux compatibility. Much additional functionality was developed to achieve the specific outputs required by this research. The code was then completely overhauled in April 2017 to make it more adaptive. This enabled the automatic data file retrieval and processing of multi-day plots, as well as features such as zooming. The inputs, outputs, and structure of the ISM script is discussed below.

Header & Setup

In compliance with good programming practices, each script begins with a full top-matter introduction section (commented), explaining the purpose of the code, the high-level inputs required, the function calls employed, a full change-log, and authorship details. A setup section follows, where variables and inputs are defined. The inputs for the ISM script include:

- File paths for functions and external scripts
- Data file paths, specific to ISM/PSN and AGLS2/GOUGH
- Output file paths
- Location labels for this particular script (AGLS2 or GOUGH)

- Required START date and time
- Required END date and time
- PRN Highlighting option (to focus on a specific satellite)
- The GPS Epoch information (13 January 1980)
- Thresholds:
    - Elevation cut-off (degrees): 0 (see Section 3.3)
    - S_4 lower limit: 0.05 (value used by SANSA for other scintillation studies)
    - S_4 upper limit: 30 (see Section 4.1 for explanation)
    - σ_ϕ lower limit (radians): 0.05 (consistency with S_4)

Flags

This section provides flexibility by allowing the user to choose between a variety of options by toggling a series of flags on or off (0 is off - code is ignored, 1 is on - code is run). Detailed information on the function of each flag is provided through comments in the software.

- Show/hide a variety of labels on the output graphs
- Select whether to highlight a specific PRN
- Choose whether to suppress data from Geostationary GPS satellites
- Select which graphs the user wishes to generate (12 different sets available)
- Select between degrees and radians
- Indicate whether temporary files should be deleted at the end of processing

Read Data & Time Calculations

The first task performed by the script is to check whether the START and END times run over more than one day. The script then finds the appropriate daily/hourly data files for the required period. The data can be in either `*.ism` or `*.txt` formats, or can take the form of a `*.mat` file. This is a binary MATLAB data file which was generated during a previous run of the code using the same dates (and not deleted after use).

The code then performs the necessary time conversions and calculations (such as GPS time to UTC) in order to limit the data arrays to only the selected range; Users can specify the time down to the second. For an ISM script, the data read from the file is found in columns 1, 2, 3, 5, 6, 7, 8, 9, 14, 23, 19, 20, and 25 (in that order). MATLAB uses a base index of 1; it does not count from 0 when specifying array indices.

Lastly, using the selected time range information, the script can auto-generate titles (for plotting graphs) and filenames (for saving graph outputs).

Analytics & Graph Generation

The following sections of code handle all the algorithms and graph plotting (in the order listed). The numbers shown below are the unique filename IDs of the various output graphs and were used to group the files together.

- 10 - Plot Raw S_4
- 20 - Plot Raw σ_ϕ (case: radians, upper limit: 30)
- 1 - Plot SNR (1 PRN)
- 2 - Plot L1 Lock Time (ALL PRN) and Elevation (ALL PRN) (2-panel)
- 3 - Plot L1 Lock Time (1 PRN) and Elevation (1 PRN) (2-panel)
- Calculate and apply S_4 Correction (using Equation 2.6)
- Removal of outliers (S_4 and σ_ϕ)
- 50 - Plot Elevation and Azimuth (ALL PRN) satellite visibility map
- Remove anomalous PRNs, Remove low elevation data
- 13 - Plot Corrected S_4 (ALL PRN)
- Filter and clean for Corrected σ_ϕ, remove anomalous data
- 23 - Plot Corrected σ_ϕ (ALL PRN)
- 24 - Plot Corrected σ_ϕ (1 PRN)
- 25 - Plot Corrected S_4 (1 PRN)
- 11 - Plot 32-panel S_4-Elevation map
- 22 - Plot 32-panel σ_ϕ-Elevation map
- 30 - Slant TEC (ALL PRN)
- Calculate Vertical TEC using Function `slm2.m` with h = 350 km.
- Calculate Mean VTEC using polynomial fit, adjust min VTEC by 5 TECU
- 31 - Plot Vertical TEC (ALL PRN)

Housekeeping

The final section of MATLAB code performs fundamental housekeeping tasks to bring the program to a close. These actions include:

- Clearing variables in preparation of new run
- Deleting temporary data files (to save space)
- Saving processed ISM data to a text file
- Closing open files and resetting file paths
- Print confirmation of successful script run

A.2.2 MATLAB: PSN scripts

As with the MATLAB ISM script, the foundation code for the PSN script was provided by Dr Pierre Cilliers (Microsoft Windows version). This ensured that the methodology and formulas used to process the position data and produce the maps were from a verified source. The PSN code was first adapted for Linux compatibility, and much additional functionality was added. The code was also completely revised to make it adaptive, allowing for automatic data file identification and retrieval when generating maps which required data from multiple days.

A freely available mapping toolbox for MATLAB, called m_map (Pawlowicz, 2018) was implemented in the PSN scripts to generate the map content. Two versions of the PSN script were created: one for the SA Agulhas II data, and one for the Gough Island data. This was necessary because the position error calculations differ between a stationary GPS receiver and a moving GPS receiver. The methodology of the position error calculation is discussed in Section 4.6.

Header & Setup

The top matter of the PSN script contains an introduction to the purpose of the script, authorship, and a full revision history of added functionality and fixes. An input section follows, where the following information is entered:

- File paths for functions and external scripts
- Data file paths for input data and output files
- Map projection option: 'Miller' or 'Satellite' (Miller was used)
- Map centre latitude and longitude (for Miller projection)
- Earth radius value (we used R_e = '6378e3' meters)
- Required START date and time
- Required END date and time

Flags

The following flags are available in the setup of the PSN script, allowing the user to select between a variety of functional options by toggling them on (1) or off (0):

- Select which graphs the user wishes to generate (7 sets available)
- Choose whether to save processed data to a *.mat file
- Indicate whether to automatically save the output plots to the results file
- Choose whether to show fixed SANSA GISTM locations on the world map

Read Data & Time Calculations

The first task is to check whether the START and END times run over more than one day. The script then finds the appropriate PSN data files for the required period. The script searches for an existing *.mat data file which spans the selected period. If one is present, it is used instead of reading in the data from a *.psn file. Unlike the ISM files, the PSN file is in plain text format, and is human-readable. A MAT file is binary and loads quicker into the MATLAB scripts.

The time information in the PSN data file is already presented in UTC in a standard format. The data arrays are then limited to only the selected time range. All of the columns are read into the data file; the number of columns in an entry can vary depending on the number of satellites being tracked. The script auto-generates titles and output filenames for the graphs.

Analytics & Graph Generation

Several calculations are performed and graphs are plotted in the next section of code. The numbers indicate the unique filename ID of the various graphs. The script performs the following steps in sequential order:

- 88 - Plot Position values on a world map (15-minute intervals)
- Calculate mean position and position errors (running mean or stationary mean)
- Calculate error statistics
- Identify and highlight 20 largest Horizontal errors
- 991, 992, 993 - Plot Horizontal, Vertical, and Absolute error histograms
- 994 - Plot Latitude, Longitude, Altitude versus Time (3-panel, coordinates)
- 58 - Plot Velocity versus Time
- 995 - Plot Δ(Absolute), Δ(Horizontal), Δ(Altitude) versus Time (3-panel, meters)
- 996 - Plot Position scatterplot (coordinates) –AND–
- 997 - Plot Δ(Position) scatterplot (meters)
- 87 - Plot Δ(Horizontal error), Number of Locked Satellites versus Time (2-panel, meters)

Housekeeping

The PSN script does not have a dedicated housekeeping section. Instead, saving processed data to a *.mat MATLAB binary data file only occurs if that flag has been selected, and takes place before the arrays are limited to only the selected period. Variables are cleared as needed throughout the code. Confirmation of script success is limited to a single print statement at the end of the program as individual plots and saving of the plots carry their own confirmation messages.

Aarons, J. (1993), 'The longitudinal morphology of equatorial F-Layer irregularities relevant to their occurrence', *Space Science Reviews* **63**(3-4), 209–243.

Atilaw, T. Y., Cilliers, P. J. and Martinez, P. (2015), Characterization of the Multipath Environment of Ionospheric Scintillation Receivers, Master's book, University of Cape Town.
URL: *https://open.uct.ac.za/handle/11427/16475*

Azeem, I., Crowley, G. and Reynolds, A. (2015), First Measurements of Ionospheric TEC and GPS Scintillations from an Unmanned Marine Vehicle, *in* 'Proceedings of the 14th International Ionospheric Effects Symposium, 12-14 May 2015, Alexandria, VA, USA'.
URL: *http://ies2015.bc.edu/wp-content/uploads/2015/05/144-Azeem-Paper.pdf*

Azeem, I., Crowley, G. and Reynolds, A. (2016), Towards Ionospheric TEC and GPS Scintillation Monitoring from the Oceanic Region, *in* '19th International Beacon Satellite Symposium, BSS-2016 The Abdus Salam ICTP, Trieste Italy, 28 June 2016'.
URL: *https://t-ict4d.ictp.it/beacon2016/program-overview*

Badke, B. (2009), 'GNSS Solutions: What is C/N_o and how is it calculated in a GNSS receiver?', *InsideGNSS* **5**, 20–23.
URL: *http://insidegnss.com/wp-content/uploads/2018/01/sepoct09-gnss-sol.pdf*

Basu, S., Groves, K. M., Basu, S. and Sultan, P. J. (2002), 'Specification and forecasting of scintillations in communication/navigation links: Current status and future plans', *Journal of Atmospheric and Solar-Terrestrial Physics* **64**(16), 1745–1754.

Beary, T. (2014), 'GPS GDOP 4 satellites Poor' and 'GPS GDOP 4 satellites Good', *in* 'TMJBeary's Clipart: GPS DOP Gallery', Openclipart.org.
URL: *https://openclipart.org/user-detail/tmjbeary*

Carrano, C. and Groves, K. (2009), Presentation: Remote Sensing the Ionosphere Using GPS-SCINDA, *in* 'IHY-AFRICA/SCINDA Workshop Zambia 2009', Livingstone, Zambia.
URL: *https://slideplayer.com/slide/4903794/*

Carrano, C., Groves, K. and Griffin, J. (2005), Empirical characterization and modeling of GPS positioning errors due to ionospheric scintillation, *in* 'Proceedings of the Ionospheric Effects

Symposium, Alexandria, VA, May 3 - 5', Alexandria, VA.
URL: *https://bit.ly/2Aa1ykl*

Cilliers, P. J., Mitchell, C. N. and Opperman, B. D. L. (2006), Characterization of the Ionosphere over the South Atlantic Ocean by Means of Ionospheric Tomography using Dual Frequency GPS Signals Received On Board a Research Ship, *in* 'Proceedings of NATO Information Systems Technology (IST) Panel Specialists Meeting on Characterising the Ionosphere, Fairbanks, RTO-MP-IST-056', pp. 1–18.

Cozzens, T. (2017), 'Broadcom launches dual-frequency receiver for mass market'.
URL: *http://gpsworld.com/broadcom-launches-dual-frequency-gnss-receiver-for-mass-market/*

Damm, W. (2010), 'Signal-to-Noise, Carrier-to-Noise, EbNo: on Signal Quality Ratios', *in* 'NoiseCom Resource Library: Webinars', Noisecom.
URL: *http://www.noisecom.com/resource-library/webinars/sn-cn-ebno-webinar*

Doherty, P. H., Delay, S. H., Valladares, C. E. and Klobuchar, J. A. (2003), 'Ionospheric scintillation effects on GPS in the equatorial and auroral regions', *Navigation* **50**(4), 235–245.

Du, J., Caruana, J., Wilkinson, P., Thomas, R. and Cervera, M. (2000), Determination of Equatorial Ionospheric Scintillation S_4 by Dual Frequency GPS, *in* 'Proceedings WARS'00: Workshop on Applications of Radio Science, 27-29 April, La Trobe University Melbourne', pp. 85–90.
URL: *http://www.sws.bom.gov.au/IPSHosted/NCRS/wars/wars2000/commg/du.pdf*

Forte, B. and Radicella, S. (2002), 'Problems in data treatment for ionospheric scintillation measurements', *Radio Science* **37**(6), 8.1–8.5.
URL: *https://agupubs.onlinelibrary.wiley.com/doi/abs/10.1029/2001RS002508*

Freeman, R. L. (1981), Chapter 1.10: Signal-to-Noise Ratio, *in* 'Telecommunications Transmission Handbook, 2nd Ed.', John Wiley & Sons, Inc.

Georges, T. (1969), 'Effects of Ionospheric Motions and Irregularities on HF Radio Propagation', *Low-Frequency Waves and Irregularities in the Ionosphere* **14**, 137–151.
URL: *https://doi.org/10.1007/978-94-010-3402-9_11*

Ghoddousi-Fard, R., Prikryl, P. and Lahaye, F. (2013), 'GPS phase difference variation statistics: A comparison between phase scintillation index and proxy indices', *Advances in Space Research* **52**, 1397–1405.

Google Earth (2017), 'Google Earth Satellite Image overlaid with SA Agulhas II GPS Data'. Accessed 18-05-2017.
URL: *goo.gl/maps/GcXuHjkdpbm*

GPSWorld (2007), 'White House Agrees to Remove Selective Availability'.
  URL: *http://gpsworld.com/defensenewswhite-house-agrees-remove-selective-availability-3243/*

Habarulema, J. B., McKinnell, L.-A., Cilliers, P. J. and Opperman, B. D. (2009), 'Application of neural networks to South African GPS TEC modelling', *Advances in Space Research* **43**(11), 1711–1720.

Hartmann, G. A. and Pacca, I. G. (2009), 'Time evolution of the South Atlantic Magnetic Anomaly', *Annals of the Brazilian Academy of Sciences (AABC)* **81**(2), 243–255.
  URL: *http://www.scielo.br/pdf/aabc/v81n2/v81n2a10.pdf*

Hofmann-Wellenhof, B., Lichtenegger, H. and Collins, J. (2001), *Global Positioning System: Theory and Practice 5th Ed.*, Springer.

Horvath, I. and Crozier, S. (2007), 'Software developed for obtaining GPS-derived total electron content values', *Radio Science* **42**(RS2002), 1–20.
  URL: *https://agupubs.onlinelibrary.wiley.com/doi/pdf/10.1029/2006RS003452*

IETF (2018), 'IETF leap-seconds.list update 05 July 2018 via IERS Bulletin C55', *Internet Engineering Task Force: Leap Seconds List* **C55**.
  URL: *https://www.ietf.org/timezones/data/leap-seconds.list*

Jewell, D. (2007), 'GPS Insights: Looking Aft, Looking Fore'.
  URL: *http://gpsworld.com/gps-insights-looking-aft-looking-fore/*

Jiao, Y., Morton, Y. T., Taylor, S. and Pelgrum, W. (2013), 'Characterization of high-latitude ionospheric scintillation of GPS signals', *Radio Science* **48**(6), 698–708.

Joseph, A. (2010), 'Measuring GNSS Signal Strength: What is the difference between SNR and C/N_0?', *InsideGNSS* **6**, 20–25.
  URL: *http://insidegnss.com/wp-content/uploads/2018/01/novdec10-Solutions.pdf*

Kintner, P. M., Humphreys, T. and Hinks, J. (2009), 'GNSS and ionospheric scintillation', *Inside GNSS* **4**, 22–30.
  URL: *http://www.insidegnss.com/auto/julyaug09-kintner.pdf*

Kintner, P. M., Ledvina, B. M. and de Paula, E. R. (2007), 'GPS and ionospheric scintillations', *Space Weather* **5**.
  URL: *http://doi.wiley.com/10.1029/2006SW000260*

Kirienko, Y. (2007), 'Ionospheric Pierce Point - File Image: IPP.svg'.
  Accessed 27-09-2018.
  URL: *https://commons.wikimedia.org/wiki/File:IPP.svg*

Klobuchar, J. A. (1987), 'Ionospheric time-delay algorithm for single-frequency GPS users', *IEEE Transactions on Aerospace and Electronic Systems* **AES-23**(3), 325–331.

Korte, M., Mandea, M., Linthe, H., Hemshorn, A., Kotzé, P. and Ricaldi, E. (2009), 'New geomagnetic field observations in the South Atlantic Anomaly region', *Ann.Geophys* **52**(1), 65–81.

Kyoto Geomagnetic World Data Centre (2015), 'Plot and data output of Mid-latitude Geomagnetic Indices ASY/SYM and AE for 15 - 28 September 2015'.
Accessed 02-04-2017.
URL: *http://wdc.kugi.kyoto-u.ac.jp/aeasy/index.html*

Langley, R. B. (1999), 'Dilution of Precision', *GPS World: Innovation* **5**, 52–59.
URL: *http://www2.unb.ca/gge/Resources/gpsworld.may99.pdf*

Lenz, P. and Breger, M. (2010), 'Period04 v1.2.0'.
URL: *https://www.univie.ac.at/tops/Period04/*

Lilla, D. and Potgieter, H. (2015), SANSA Space Science: SANAE Polar Space Weather Studies - Month End Report September 2015, Technical report, South African National Space Agency, SANSA Space Science, 1 Hospital Street, Hermanus, South Africa.

McNamara, L. (1991), *The Ionosphere: Communications, Surveillance, and Direction Finding*, Krieger Publishing Company.

Muella, M., de Paula, E. and Jonah, O. (2014), 'GPS L1-frequency observations of equatorial scintillations and irregularity zonal velocities', *Surveys in Geophysics* **35**, 335–357.

NOAA (2018), 'GPS.gov: The Global Positioning System - Overview'.
Accessed 06-03-2018.
URL: *http://www.gps.gov/systems/gps/*

NovAtel (2015), 'An Introduction to GNSS: GPS, GLONASS, BeiDou, Galileo and other Global Navigation Satellite Systems'.
URL: *https://www.novatel.com/an-introduction-to-gnss/*

Pawlowicz, R. (2018), 'M_Map: A mapping package for MATLAB'.
URL: *www.eoas.ubc.ca/~rich/map.html*

Peng, S. and Morton, Y. (2011), 'High Latitude Ionosphere Scintillations at GPS L5 Band', pp. 597–607.
URL: *https://www.ion.org/publications/abstract.cfm?articleID=9621*

Powers, E. (2017), GPS Week Roll Over Issue, *in* '57th Meeting of the Civil GPS Service Interface Committee, 25-26 September 2017', USNO/GPS.gov, Portland, Oregon.
URL: *https://www.gps.gov/cgsic/meetings/2017/powers.pdf*

Robins, R. E., Secan, J. A. and Fremouw, E. J. (1986), A mid-latitude scintillation model, Technical report, Northwest Research Associates, Inc., Bellevue, WA.
URL: *http://www.dtic.mil/dtic/tr/fulltext/u2/a183143.pdf*

SA Dep. of Environmental Affairs (2018), 'SA Agulhas II & Islands'.
Accessed January 2018.
URL: *https://www.environment.gov.za/sites/default/files/docs/publications/SA_agulhas.pdf*

Sailwx (2015), 'SA Agulhas II - ZSNO - position and weather'.
URL: *https://www.sailwx.info/shiptrack/shipposition.phtml?call=ZSNO*

SBAS Ionospheric Working Group (2010), Effect of Ionospheric Scintillations on GNSS - A White Paper, Technical report, Stanford University Engineering GPS Lab.
URL: *http://web.stanford.edu/group/scpnt/gpslab/website_files/sbas-ion_wg/sbas_iono_scintillations_white_paper.pdf*

Skone, S., Knudsen, K. and De Jong, M. (2001), 'Limitations in GPS receiver tracking performance under ionospheric scintillation conditions', *Physics and Chemistry of the Earth, Part* .
URL: *http://www.sciencedirect.com/science/article/pii/S1464189501001107*

Spogli, L., Alfonsi, L, C. P. J., Correia, E., De Franceschi, G., Mitchell, C. N., Romano, V., Kinrade, J. and Cabrera, M. A. (2013), 'GPS scintillations and total electron content climatology in the southern low, middle and high latitude regions', *Annals of Geophysics* **56**(2).

Trimble (2018), 'GNSS Planning Online'.
URL: *https://www.gnssplanning.com/*

van der Merwe, S. J. (2011), Characterisation of the ionosphere over the South Atlantic Anomaly by using a ship-based dual-frequency GPS receiver, Master's book, University of Pretoria.

Van Dierendonck, A. J. (2009), GSV4004B GPS Ionospheric Scintillation & TEC Monitor (User's Manual), Technical report, AJ Systems/GPS Silicon Valley, AJ Systems/GPS Silicon Valley, Los Altos, California.
URL: *http://indico.ictp.it/event/a08148/session/90/contribution/56/material/0/0.pdf*

Van Dierendonck, A. J., Klobuchar, J. and Hua, Q. (1993), 'Ionospheric Scintillation Monitoring Using Commercial Single Frequency C/A Code Receivers', pp. 1333–1342.

Vermeulen, A., Cilliers, P. and Martinez, P. (2016), 'Ionospheric characterisation of the South Atlantic Magnetic Anomaly using a mobile ship-based dual-frequency GPS Ionospheric Scintillation and Total Electron Content Monitor', *The Proceedings of SAIP2016, the 61st Annual Conference of the South African Institute of Physics* pp. 331–335.
URL: *http://events.saip.org.za/internalPage.py?pageId=10&confId=86*

Wang, Y., Zhang, Q., Jayachandran, P. T., Lockwood, M., Zhang, S. R., Moen, J., Xing, Z. Y., Ma, Y. Z. and Lester, M. (2016), 'A comparison between large-scale irregularities and scintillations in the polar ionosphere', *Geophysical Research Letters* **43**(10), 4790–4798.

Wanliss, J. A. and Showalter, K. M. (2006), 'High-resolution global storm index: Dst versus SYM-H', *Journal of Geophysical Research* **111**(A02202).
URL: *http://doi.wiley.com/10.1029/2005JA011034 http://onlinelibrary.wiley.com/doi/10.1029/2005JA0*

Wernik, A. W., Secan, J. A. and Fremouw, E. J. (2003), 'Ionospheric irregularities and scintillation', *Advances in Space Research* **31**(4), 971–981.

Wikimedia Commons (2007), 'Map of Gough Island - File Image: Gough.png'. Accessed 08-04-2016.
URL: *https://commons.wikimedia.org/wiki/File:Gough.png*

Yuen, M. F., Driels, M. R. and Harkins, R. M. (2009), Dilution Of Precision (DOP) Calculation for Mission Planning Purposes, Master's book, Naval Postgraduate School.
URL: *https://calhoun.nps.edu/handle/10945/4810*